"I am quite im   *the*
life of the Cana   nory
lane it was for   *life*
of the penny today. The use of characters to share the history was very well done. I really appreciated the inclusion of some of the household uses of the penny; some of which I had heard of and others I had not. I remember seeing pennies get flattened on the train tracks, which during my years, was considered an innocent game.

Throughout the book I was able to get to know the penny personally. Susan brings the penny, called "Copper" to life, and enabled me to look at the "lowly" penny in a completely different light. I also found the facts and "games" to be very intriguing and thought provoking. The inclusions of these items, as well as the many facts of the penny, certainly give the book an educational factor.

I could see this book becoming a resource for schools, in particular in grade 5 Social Studies, as the Saskatchewan curriculum at that grade level deals with Canada. This book could also be used at the grade 12 level in Canadian Studies. The inclusion of the chemical composition would allow chemistry teachers to utilize it and the rounding facts would fit well in a math lesson.

Due to the significance of the penny's retirement, I would recommend that this book be placed in every school library in Canada, as it would allow readers to trace and follow the history of the penny from its inception to its retirement. The penny is something that may be gone, but should not be forgotten due to its place in Canadian history and development.

I was pleased to have the opportunity to review this book, so much so that I've pre-ordered copies for all the schools in Good Spirit School Division."

ALAN SHARP

Superintendent of Program Development
Good Spirit School Division
Yorkton, Saskatchewan, Canada

"This book, *little copper pennies - Celebrating the life of the Canadian one cent piece (1858-2013)*, brings to the forefront things that have been taken for granted for most of the penny's life - its history, uses and factual heritage. These aspects have been sidelined in face of the penny losing its currency value and purchasing power.

Susan Harris has connected with the true essence of the penny beyond its monetary value. She has skillfully woven humour, nostalgia and factual expressions into simple stories we can easily identify with in our own lives, and appreciate in the lives of others. Her brand of storytelling takes us on penny-journeys from its inception to present, the year of the final minting of the coin. She effectively articulates the benefits as well as the reasons for discontinuing the circulation of the penny.

As an educator for approximately thirteen years, having to understand and apply knowledge to make the abstract a reality, a paradigm shift occurred whilst I read this book. I will never view the penny as insignificant or intangible again! Whether you are Canadian or not, you will be inspired to view your country's lowest currency through fresh lens. The penny has a powerful legacy that is just waiting to unfold...read and see for yourself."

KAREN BEEKEE

B.Sc. Mathematics
Teacher, 1995-2009

little copper pennies

··

CELEBRATING THE LIFE OF THE
CANADIAN ONE-CENT PIECE
(1858-2013)

··

SUSAN HARRIS

Terry,

Keep the memories alive

Susan Harris

Visit Susan Harris website at http://www.susanharris.ca

www.facebook.com/goldensusanharris

Susan Harris @SusanHarris20 on Twitter

On July 30, 2012 it was announced that pennies will be remain in circulation until February 4, 2013.

All composition pie charts were created by the author.

Penny images show only the reverse (design) side.

Some personalities are real and some are created to depict the facts, events and environments which are historically accurate. Names have been changed.

Cataloguing data available from Library and Archives Canada.

ISBN 978-1-4602-0468-9

Dedication

To Tim,

my sounding board
and penny lover.

Acknowledgements

I am humbly grateful to be invited into the lives of the many individuals, friends and relatives who regaled me with tales of the years gone by, and their fun uses of the penny. Many thanks to them all.

To Karen for the proficient editing of this book in less than one week, and for setting aside her busy schedule to review and read several times over, I owe a huge thank you. I value her contribution as a formal educator, and appreciate the prayers and blessings on my endeavour.

Thanks to the Royal Canadian Mint for access to the website content and facts, and for permission to use their Intellectual Property in the form of the penny images.

Thanks to CBC Canada for permission to use their broadcasting article as an appendix in this book.

I thank Don Wihak, computer literacy teacher at Melville Comprehensive School, for his technical expertise with the image requirements. Without his kind assistance, this book would have been delayed.

Special thanks to Bob Lindsay for the many stories and memories he provided, some of which are recorded in single chapters while others are sprinkled throughout the book.

I thank my husband and daughter for patiently understanding my need to write and for believing in what I was writing. Their excitement, unflagging support and feedback sustained the momentum needed to create this work in a short time frame. Thanks to Tim for the stories he shared, the contacts he made for interviews and for his knowledge of Canadian culture and history.

Thanks to Radiance for taking care of her school work, helping at home and understanding that she could not have friends over while I wrote. Best of all, she is the prototype of the next generation that will not use pennies, and the knowledge and appreciation of the past through the research for this book, will strengthen her Canadian legacy. Thanks also for taking the photo on the back cover.

Above all, I thank God for blessing this book to fruition, and for my own experiences which are contained therein.

Contents

CHAPTER 1

BAD NEWS

The month of March brings anticipation of spring, daylight saving time, glorious colours of tulips and lilies, and airports jammed with families escaping for school break. For the little penny, March was significant for another reason.

There had been far too many groups discussing its existence for years now. They had done a study on its future and the implications did not look promising. True, there were many who favoured its presence, for practical as well as sentimental reasons. It had worth. It is history. Then there was the other crowd that found it useless. The real significance however, was that in many parts of the world, its peers had been eliminated, and this had become the worst nightmare of the tiny coin's life.

To put it candidly, the penny was losing its value. The purchasing power of its one-cent piece was nil. Since the investigation, the penny trembled, knowing it was living on borrowed time. You can call it crazy but the little coin wanted to stay. It suspected the worst and so did not want the calendar to move ahead. Least of all, it never expected that in the season of spring when life bursts from every source, the epitaph of its death would be written. There it was laid for the world to read: "Elimination of the penny."

The little coin did not have blue eyes or light skin, or a heart. At least, not the kind you are born with. Nonetheless, it had its own special kind of heart from which it drew pain and purpose.

The penny was born, or more correctly, minted on a day that could have been sunny and bright, but maybe it was cold and foggy, even raining in London. Instead of warm body tissue heralding its entry, hot copper marked its arrival. Its name is not written with an uppercase letter like yours, as birth certificates demand, so during its adventures, it will be called Copper, with a capital C. Created a one cent piece, it was given the slang name 'penny' from its predecessor the pence, and is valued at one-hundredth of a dollar.

The penny was created to introduce change. The province of Canada as it was then called, was adopting the decimal system, and a cent coin was needed. With only about two million persons, and animals outnumbering those by multiples, Canada was the kind of nation whose infancy was marked with thrilling invasions and heroic acts. Fur traders, timber loggers and an intermingling of heritages punctuated the landscape of the little coin's new world, each striving for its conquest. Soft and cosy, the little beaver was claimed for its share of fashionable hats for eager European women. Grain was also taking off. So the little penny was excited to be the face of change for the budding dominion.

A century and a half later, the portrait of Queen Elizabeth II is embossed on the penny's face. On its reverse are two maple leaves on a twig. At 19.05 mm, weight is not an issue, and it is flawless and shiny.

little copper pennies

Though flawless only on the outside.

The eye cannot tell that that the copper coin is different, that ironically, it is only copper plated. That its value is echoed in the lower priced steel in its body.

The penny's nightmare has escalated and its special kind of heart is heavy even as its smile flashes on the gaudy surface of its elegant shape. Its tin part gone, the coin jokes that it will always be thin. Sometimes humour is the only way to endure troubled times.

"Suck it up, Gorgeous, people only look at the outside. You look good and still turn heads."

The penny didn't just turn heads. Men, women, boys and girls turned their bodies to pick it up from parking lots and floors. With the minting of pennies already finished, in the winter of 2013 distribution will cease, and the little coin will be phased out. Still, its adventures, meaning and history must not be wiped out.

Over and over the penny recounted the good days, the academics about its worth, the joys it brought, the liability it has become. The next generation will know it only as recycled metal. So before the last one is distributed on February 4, 2013, its legacy must be written.

Penny Facts

1. When pennies come out of the mint they are very shiny but become tarnished when exposed to air, chemicals, dirt and oils from human fingers.
2. The first penny produced in 1858 had a 95% copper content, while the last penny had a 4.5% copper plating only.
3. Pennies are made from melted metal rolled into flat

sheets from which discs or blanks are pressed. The discs are stamped with a die bearing images designed by an artist.

Penny Fun

- Blindfold persons and see who can pick out pennies from an assortment of coins, in a minute. You can compete singly or with a few persons at a time. The person with the most pennies wins.

- Fill a jar or can with pennies and use as an ice breaker or fun event by asking others to guess how many pennies are in the jar. Give the jar to the winner who comes closest to the correct number without going over.

CHAPTER 2

THE MAPLE LEAF

The photo standing on the end table crashed to the floor as Morley slammed the front door. The Stanley Cup finals had started and he had missed the opening. His team, the Edmonton Oilers was playing the Toronto Maple Leafs for the coveted Lord Stanley's Cup. Dunking the refill of blood pressure medication and change on the kitchen table, he didn't have to inform his grandmother that he had returned. The old lady was already shuffling out of her room with her walker, disturbed by the sound of shattering glass.

"Do you want to break down the house?" Her quavering question is rhetorical.

The little penny, Copper, lay among the $2.23 change Morley had placed on the table: a toonie coin, two dimes and three pennies. The youth was already absorbed in the game and the volume of the television drowned out any concerns his grandmother expressed. Until her knee was replaced, she could not bend down to pick up the remnants of the photo. Loud cheers and a few muffled swears emanated from the living room. Then the Oilers scored and the giddy young man made his way to the kitchen for a beer during the commercial break.

"Sorry *Kokum* (Grandmother)," he calls out to her in her native language, and stooping down, Morley picked up the shattered photo and tried to clean the mess of splinters. The face of his deceased grandfather peered back, a hole in one cheek, mutilated by the broken glass. He pressed the hole, trying to smooth it out with his fingers.

"I'll buy back a replacement frame." He gingerly pulls a triangle of the sharp object stuck in one corner.

The old lady in the armchair looks at him and says nothing.

"There was only one cashier and the line was long," the young man explains, as if feeling guilty by her silence. "Of course these customers just have to pay with pennies."

He shook his head as if baffled at the seeming indifferent nature of people to the Stanley finals that was starting in five minutes. Not once did he allude to Kokum's last minute request for her medication refill.

"I don't know why they have to hold up everyone else to get those pennies. I'm not going to miss that thing when it's gone." Morley offers the explanation as it pained him to see his grandmother so sad.

He loved Kokum with her long hair and brown, lined face. He wished he saw her more often, though. The photo was precious to her and she cherished her possessions. She was a hoarder too, a trait which dated back to her years growing up in poverty.

The sound of cheering fans from the television screen signalled that the game had resumed. Like most Canadians, hockey was supreme to Morley. It was well known Canadian history that more than a century ago, in

little copper pennies

1892, Lord Stanley, Canada's then governor general, had commented at a sports banquet in Ottawa.

"I have for some time been thinking that it would be a good thing if there were a challenge cup, which would be held from year to year by the leading hockey club in Canada. There does not appear to be any outward sign of a championship at present, and considering the interest that hockey matches now elicit, I am willing to give a cup which shall be held annually by the winning club."

The following year, the son of Preston kept true to his word. Purchasing a silver bowl for $50, he named it the Dominion Hockey Challenge Cup. Fans gave it the less formal designation of the Stanley Cup.[1]

Near three hours later, and an Oiler's victory, Morley sat down with Kokum for a simple supper of Indian taco. This was his favourite dish, bannock (fried bread) topped with ground beef served with all the toppings of taco - tomatoes, lettuce, mayo, cheese and onions. Tomorrow his grandmother was going in for knee surgery, and he was staying over so he could drive her to the hospital, after which his sister would take over the rest of her care.

Kokum toyed with the coins on the table and then spoke. "So you'd be glad to see the penny go." Her remark was more of a statement than a question. "A penny is precious Morley," she continued. "It has the maple leaf on it."

Morley knew generally that all coins carried a symbol of Canada on one side, but he did not give active thought to the respective symbols each had. Kokum picked up Copper and held its reverse towards Morley. Not one, but two maple leaves on a twig, decorated its side.

"Uh huh." He murmured, biting into delicious ground beef and fried bread. Kokum's knees may need replacing but there was nothing to replace when it came to her cooking.

"Our ancestors discovered the maple syrup from the trees, Morley. Long before the French people came, our people gathered maple sap from the trees every year in spring, and made it into sugar. The syrup sweetened their food and was also used for their medicine. Then when the French came, our people showed them how to get the sap."

The stories had been passed on to Kokum from her elders and she was never tired of recounting the episodes.

One popular legend on how the maple sap was discovered tells of a native chief who supposedly hurled his tomahawk at a tree. The tree happened to be a maple, and sap began to flow. The clear liquid that dropped from the gash was collected in a container that chanced to be on the ground below. The chief's wife, believing the liquid was water, used it to cook venison. Once cooked, the meat and the gravy were found to be unusually delicious. Retracing how this occurred, it was revealed that the sweet sap from the maple tree was the only difference.[2]

Morley was only listening with half an ear to the tale today. Maple sap was a fresh food after the long dead winter, but his interest in the syrup laid more in consuming it for breakfast on pancakes, waffles, oatmeal or porridge. However, he was truly remorseful over breaking the photo, so he feigned interest to make up for his blunder. If asked, he would confess that Kokum was very wise, and her advice would be akin to a library book.

"Good thing they got the maple before anyone else, Kokum."

He took a second bannock and spread it with beef. Placing lettuce and tomatoes on the mince, he completed the taco with another slice of the delicious bread. Kokum seemed to have lost her appetite in the interest of passing on knowledge to her grandson.

"And hundreds of years ago, the maple leaf became known as the best Canadian symbol…"

She trailed off and Morley poured some pop in a glass to wash down the bannock.

This was long ago, but the history books showed that before the 1700s, the maple leaf was already making its mark as a Canadian symbol. Copper was interested to know the heritage of the leaves embossed on its reverse.

Kokum resumed her discourse. "They made a song about the maple leaf for Confederation."

This was also true. Alexander Muir, songwriter and school principal, wrote the song, *The Maple Leaf Forever* as Canada's confederation song in 1867, when the country was formed. For several decades it was regarded as the national song.[3]

Morley drew his eyebrows together. He did not know about the song, and was very surprised that his unschooled grandma knew so much. He would check on Confederation when he returned home, as Kokum did not have a computer to do the research immediately.

With new respect and genuine interest, he asked, "What else has the maple leaf done?"

"The flag," was the simple answer. "It waves on our flag, like the crow flying in the sky."

In 1965, the maple leaf became the most prominent symbol of Canada when the National Flag was inaugurated, a red leaf on a white background. The green maple leaves usually turned bright red in the fall, a change that results from food trapped in its leaves. When the leaves stop making food and sunlight is decreased, the green chlorophyll goes away, exposing additional colours in the underlying yellow or orange pigment. This Morley knew.

People often parallel their experiences to what is happening externally. It appeared that to the aging woman, removing the penny meant more than stopping production of a coin. It was sentiment born from grassroots survival, struggles and displacement. The aboriginal people, now called First Nations, were the pioneers and predecessors of the life giving sap from the trees whose leaves turned gorgeous red in autumn.

Autumn. The same season when pennies that bore the maple leaves were originally destined to cease being distributed in Canada. Then the penny's life had been extended until the winter of 2013. Winter. The time when sap lies dormant in the bare trees, waiting to flow in spring.

At the same time the penny will go dormant forever...

Kokum looked at Copper, and so did Morley. Giving a penny for her thoughts, was it that every time her eyes fell on a one cent coin, she saw the livelihood of her people? Maple sap for food, medicine, enjoyment. Its secret they had passed on to the French in exchange for iron kettles, new knowledge and improved technology.

The significance of the maple to the First Nations people possibly transcends that of every other group that belonged to Canada. Now those reminders would be fewer and fewer, as little pennies make their way to the banks in the new year.

To be retired, like her.

To be displaced, like she would be in a few years.

little copper pennies

For one cent pieces, the final minting was done on May 4, 2012, and once they got sent to the bank next winter, they'd be returned to the mint to be melted and the metal recycled.

Forgotten.

Morley touched Copper in his grandmother's palm and stared long and hard. His firm skin was a stark contrast to her wrinkled fingers, as he covered her hand that held the little penny. Like the life messages the elders passed on to the youth in everyday, simple living, his paradigm had shifted. It was not easy to identify the emotions on his face, but there seemed to be an unspoken commitment to champion the grassroots like she did. To appreciate the history in the coins' brown faces, similar in colour to the faces of his ancestors. Round and bright like the sun.

Copper was the only brown coin with maple leaves in the money system, and the most easily identifiable. One hundred and fifty four years have passed since the leaf was immortalized in copper. Over that time, an even greater number of ethnicities had made their home in Canada. Thinking of it, a large percentage of that population also had strong feelings towards pennies and the patriotic maple leaf. In the ongoing debates, many struggle with economics over sentiment, but sentiment lies in history, and some things cannot be measured in dollars.

As for Copper, it must accept its fate, and be satisfied with the glorious years it served its country. For to serve and be removed is far more desirable than to have never served at all.

Penny Facts

1. In 1867, the penny became legal tender in the four

provinces that signed the Confederation Act: Ontario, Quebec, New Brunswick and Nova Scotia.

2. In 1937, artist G.E. Kruger-Gray created the 'two maple leaves on a twig' design on the one cent coin.

3. In 1967, the one-cent coin with a rock dove, a symbol of spiritual values and peace, was minted to commemorate the 100th anniversary of the Confederation of 1867.

Penny Fun

- Play penny pitch. Draw a circle on a smooth surface and give each competitor equal numbers of pennies. Standing at a distance, flick pennies into the circle. You can knock out your competitors' pennies if your pennies hit theirs. The winner is the first person who gets the most pennies into the circle.

- Share with a child, visitor or immigrant a bit of culture and history displayed on the penny, emphasizing the maple leaf, the Queen, the year of minting, the proper name of "cent" and colloquial name of "penny".

CHAPTER 3

IN THE FOUNTAIN

Weaving his way around strollers and shoppers, Jonathan strode toward the middle of the mall where the dome shaped peak shone with pale sunlight coming through the glass roof. Pulling out a wallet from his blue jeans, he took a penny out. It was Copper.

From the distance it looked crowded. Jonathan's 5-feet 11-inch frame towered above most of the women and youth around him, people he did not seem to notice. Neither did he pay attention to the sweet smell of the caramel store with its long lines of laughing teens. Palm trees and exotic flowers embellished the tiled area he was moving towards.

Stopping in front of the greenery, Jonathan turned Copper over in his hand. Around him, elderly men sat on the benches, fascinated by the sprays that flashed red and indigo. A couple, with arms entwined around each other's waists, whispered and then giggled, but the sounds were lost in in the roar of the shooting waters.

The fountain was spectacular. The central water jet shot eighty feet in the air, and the cascading droplets of glittering mist settled on those who stood closest. Smaller sprays of varying heights surrounded it, like obedient pages to a haughty mistress. As with a prism, little ripples danced blue, green and orange on the frothy points of the magnificent water. Against the backdrop of an azure sky, seats and paved steps held a captive audience.

Then it happened. Stretching his hand, Jonathan spun Copper into the swirling foam. The little coin wasn't sure what to make of that gesture, because though it was thrown in, it was not in an unkind manner. On the contrary, it was gentle and sacred. As Copper sank to the bottom, it could see hundreds of other coins in the shallow water. Most were pennies like it.

Plink, plink. The eager crowd was tossing in more coins.

This was new to Copper, but some of its peers had been in the fountain for nearly two weeks. The trickling water, roaring jets and cool splashes made listening difficult. You can call it superstitious, but Copper was glued to the stories that were recounted in the basin in the heart of the fountain.

"I want my mommy to not be sick. I want her to play with me." Four year old Nathan stuttered as he threw in a penny in the moving waters.

He did not want to be rid of his treasure, but Aunt Lucy who babysat him that morning urged him to drop it. She wanted to cheer his drooping spirits, so off to the mall they had gone, and after an ice cream, they passed the fountain on the way out.

"Oh well, there's nothing to lose," she had muttered, and gave the boy a penny to make a wish.

little copper pennies

He had looked at his aunt with childlike trust, and smiled. If nothing else, he was happy for a couple of hours. A penny was a small price to pay.

Copper was wondering where all this trust came from and soon got an answer. In ancient Greece, there is a belief that a nymph ruled a source of water. Young and beautiful, the girl who was related to the gods, received offerings to keep the water supply abundant. So the coin, especially the penny, came to be known as a symbol of luck.[1] They were thrown in wishing wells too.

A story was being told of Tracy. She had been downloading some music on her brother's desktop, after seeing how quickly Alex had done it at the sleepover the weekend before. She hit Click, followed by Next, Yes and Run. Then she had selected a drive and that's when the screen went black. It remained black until Robert came home and found her in the dark closet.

"You stupid dork," he bellowed and grabbed Tracy's hair. The girl screamed in pain and cowered in the corner, but she was no match for the burly youth.

"I told you not to touch my computer," he shouted. Aiming a well-placed punch with his ham-sized fist, blood had gushed from the corner of Tracy's mouth.

She had stood with a swollen face at the dancing water side. It was her fault that she had made Robert mad. If only the computer would work again then she would not have to be kicked and punched. The waters seemed to tap a rhythm:

Don't cry Tracy, so pretty like a daisy.
Drop your penny here, and do not have
a fear.

Desperately, Tracy dropped not one, but five pennies, the wish in her heart whispered in secret. She had heard others say that if you made a wish out loud, it would not come true.

"Please let the computer work," she uttered soundlessly. Bruises aside, Tracy loved her brother even though he was mean to her. Two days later, the girl came back and dropped in five more pennies, this time in thankfulness for the dead screen that had lighted again.

Delight of delights. For so many souls, a penny is a magical little wish waiting to happen.

Pennies gave hope and Copper felt good about this. Little coins have meaning.

Plink. A coin hit Copper then slid to the left as it found its own spot. A man was wishing for his girlfriend to return, his eyes glued to the water as if willing her face to mirror back to him. Another youth wished for a snowmobile like his friend's. The lady in the black pant suit and high heels had been on a television show. Now she dropped in three pennies and walked away, her wish unspoken. Dropping pennies for good luck was a very popular practice, and it was flattering for the one-cent piece.

Questions were looming before Copper: "What happened to all the coins in the fountains? Did anyone try to steal them? What about in streams and rivers?"

Copper giggled as it thought that pennies in flowing water gave a whole new meaning to the term 'income stream.' Still, when copper and zinc seep from coins, it could be harmful to fishes. The little coin hoped there were signs asking persons to not throw coins where fishes live.

It was beginning to make sense to Copper. Jonathan had been talking about his driving test tomorrow. He came to the mall to drop the cent in the fountain and make a wish. All Copper's new friends in the fountain were also there because someone they loved used them for the special honour of making their wishes come true. Copper shivered but not from cold. The little coin was special. There is so much dignity to be used so something good would happen to a person. How the little penny hoped Jonathan would pass his test.

Copper was getting tired from all the excitement when a voice broke its reverie.

From above a female piped, "I throw pennies but not for wishes because I do not believe in legends. I throw pennies because the money is collected and given to local charities."

Another voice contradicted, "Not all go to charity. Many malls with indoor fountains take the pennies to the bank and report the earnings for themselves."

Pennies for charity. Copper and its peers together provide food for the hungry, shelter for the homeless, books and supplies for schools. Pennies are hope for those who have none. Copper had a warm feeling because in its small way it makes a difference when it's added to another penny, and another. Then they become one dollar, and then hundreds of dollars.

It did not matter if Copper belonged to the mall budget or to charity. What mattered is that the little coin and its friends are not useless. They are not dropped and forgotten. They have opportunities to be meaningful and be valued. Copper lay in its watery bed and thoughts of wishes coming true danced it to sleep.

Penny Facts

1. On January 2, 1908, the Ottawa branch of the Royal Mint opened in Canada and coins were produced locally.

2. On December 1, 1931 the Ottawa branch of the Royal Mint became a wholly owned Canadian institution, the Royal Canadian Mint.

3. Since 1975 the penny has been produced at the mint in Winnipeg, Manitoba, though the mint was officially opened in 1976. Coins for circulation are produced in Winnipeg, and special edition coins are produced in Ottawa.

Penny Fun

- Toss pennies into a pool and contest swimmers to get them.
- Use pennies to indicate the years of special occasions in scrapbooks.

CHAPTER 4

THE PENNIES IN THE LOCOMOTIVE

"Do you have a penny from when you were a boy?" Mark asked Dan as he placed two coffee drinks and donuts on the table.

The tall man shook his head. "I don't keep a lot of pennies," he admitted.

All the same, he reached for his wallet on the inside pocket of his red and white coat, and to his surprise, a single penny, Copper, tumbled out amidst other money.

"You're in luck." He turned Copper over to Mark, who held it to the light to read the year of its production. It was not as old as the man.

Dan removed the lid on his cup. The red baseball cap he was wearing backwards gave him a more youthful appearance than sixty something years of age.

"I just keep a few pennies for fixing things." This was not a surprise. Mark was familiar with Dan's expertise as a mechanic, and had heard a story or two before of his unique uses of pennies. Mark's black jacket was in sharp contrast to the orangey-gold walls of the café. The green table top that held their drinks was speckled with fine black dots, and hollowed out on the dusty pink backrest of their chairs, in cursive letters, was the word *Robin's.*

"What is the most unique thing you have fixed with a penny?" the younger man asked Dan. Delighted by his rapt audience, Dan answered without hesitation, "The locomotive," and went on to describe a day in 1997 when he worked as a machinist on the engine of the Canadian National (CN) railway.

The CN is not just Canada's only transcontinental railway company. Spanning the Atlantic coast in Nova Scotia to the Pacific coast in British Columbia (BC), the CN offers integrated transportation services: rail, intermodal, trucking, freight forwarding, warehousing and distribution. It also serves fourteen states in the USA, and links not only the east and the west, but the Gulf Coast as well.[1]

The locomotive is the railway vehicle that provides the motive power for the train. It is powered by diesel which flows through fuel lines connected to injectors. The engine was a 16 cylinder motor that was propelled by sixteen injectors. Each injector had two fuel lines connected to it, giving a total of thirty two fuel lines.

Each injector also had a nozzle at the tip which controlled the flow of the pressurized diesel. On that day, the nozzle of one of the sixteen injectors was broken. Instead of a managed flow though a thin hole, the injector was gushing a larger quantity of unwanted fuel into the locomotive through its wider, broken nozzle. As the automotive mechanic, Dan's job was to provide emergency back-up in acute situations, and on that evening, he was required to plug the leak.

A routine enough job on any day.

little copper pennies

The train had left the station in BC and was on its way to its next major stop in Winnipeg, then to its destination in Montreal. All was fine as it passed through Alberta, but well into Saskatchewan, the crew on board phoned the station at Melville, to say there was a bad fuel leak.

The nozzle must be replaced, or at minimum, fuel lines must be plugged. If they were plugged, the diesel would not flow and the injector would not be flooded.

A quick search revealed no replacement plugs were housed in Melville, but the necessary part was available at the Winnipeg station. Only at certain stations in BC, Winnipeg and Montreal were train maintenance performed, and parts readily accessible. There was no way to get the plug to Melville that night.

The leaking injector could not be repaired.

"I was asked to do a temporary fix so the train could get to Winnipeg, but there were no spare units to fix it with," Dan reminisced. "So I got creative."

"What did you do?" Mark's curiosity was heightening. He knew it was well over 400 kilometres to the station in Winnipeg, from Melville, the smallest city in the province of Saskatchewan, located on the eastern side.

"The circumference of the fuel lines was the same size as a penny, so I unscrewed the nozzle cap of the faulty injector and placed a penny in each of the fuel line."

"Did they really fit?" Mark asked, sounding a bit breathless.

"Oh yeah, and then I screwed the cap back in place," Dan explained breezily. "The pennies plugged the lines and the fuel could not flow into the injector."

"How could the engine run if the fuel is shut off?" Mark did not quite understand. Dan who was a bit hard of hearing asked Mark to repeat the question. As he did, Mark studied Copper as if trying to gauge the diameter of the fuel lines.

Dan proceeded to explain that the other fifteen injectors were still intact, and could provide enough diesel to move the locomotive.

"I asked the crew to get the injector repaired when they arrived in Winnipeg, and to remove the pennies," he continued, scratching the grey stubble on his cheek before sipping his coffee.

Swallowing the warm beverage, the mechanic stated that he gave the incident no more thought, as trains were pulling up frequently at the CN station in Melville, and he was kept busy.

"Did the locomotive make it to Winnipeg?" Mark could not wait for the end. His eyes were translucent pools of green as he drank in the details of this brave feat. His creamy coffee and half-eaten donut laid cold in its white napkin, as was Copper lying next to it.

"Not just to Winnipeg, but to Montreal as well," was the humble reply.

Seeing Mark's quizzical expression, he added. "It was not until a few days after that I was called to my boss' office." Dan grinned, "There were two managers in the office and they were not smiling."

Though not easily fazed, Dan admitted that he got a bit worried when he realized the 'big boss' from Montreal was on speakerphone.

"I had no idea why I was called in," he shrugged. He had forgotten about his quick fix a couple days before.

It turned out that on arriving at Winnipeg, the locomotive seemed to be running fine, so the crew shuttled it off to

little copper pennies

Montreal without performing any repairs to the injector. Dan's two pennies set off for an additional two thousand kilometres, on a train with one injector down and endless cargo on board.

The Montreal station was a maintenance site, and the locomotive went in for servicing when it arrived. Servicing included checking things like the air brakes, oil samples and fuel lines. It was then that the penny plugs were discovered, and the little copper coins, now dark and tarnished with diesel, had a black suspicion cast on them.

It did not take long for the Montreal office to trace the source of the pennies. This led to Dan being summoned before his bosses in the Melville office, and while he was not expecting a 'Thank you', neither was he prepared for the query:

"Did you sabotage the locomotive?"

"I had to defend what had happened," the former CN employee recalls. "I told them that there were no plugs available and we needed to get the train to Winnipeg. I had called ahead to Winnipeg and the crew there verified that they would attend to plugging the fuel lines, or replacing the nozzle. I gave the lines my best shot, and plugged the leak with the pennies as a temporary fix."

In mechanic school, Dan had learnt lot of ways for quick fixes, and this one had paid off big time.

"Were you disciplined for the fix?" Mark had visions of grievances and time off work, or even a firing.

Fortunately, there were no negative reprisals. Dan's explanation rang true, and he joked about how one of the bosses had shaken his head and said. "Either you are crazy or you are a genius, Dan."

Here the hero of the locomotive paused, and sipped his creamy 'double double.' Coffee with two creams and two sugars.

"Did they shake your hand?" Mark asked.

Dan's humorous reply was, "Not at all, and neither did they give me back my two cents."

"Why did the Winnipeg crew not put in proper plugs?" Marked wanted to know.

"Maybe they did not want to have to explain the pennies, or maybe the locomotive was working just as well as it should be." Dan's reply was speculative.

It was the most courageous story of a penny that Copper had heard, and wished that *it* was one of the tiny coins that had plugged the line and got the CN to safety. All the same, Copper was proud to be a penny.

Proud to be Canadian.

Proud of what Dan had done for the national carrier.

Mark was impressed, and anxious to hear more, so he questioned the senior gentleman. "Will you miss the penny when it's gone?"

"Not me." The cheerful answer was surprising. "I think the penny became a nuisance around 1975 or so. I keep them in my car on the dash and it fills up so quickly. You can't really get anything in 2012 for a penny, like we used to when I was a kid. But what I really use the penny for is fixing things."

It was a bittersweet moment for Copper. A penny could be a hero or a nuisance, or maybe both at the same time, depending on someone's mood.

Mechanic Dan would miss the pennies primarily for its household uses. He narrated to Mark that in bathrooms

little copper pennies

and kitchens, he had stopped the flow of water in broken lines using a penny to quench the gush. Later, the families would obtain the proper part and the plumber would do his job. He said he chose copper because it bends fairly easily.

"Have you used the penny on farm equipment?" Mark too was raised on a farm and any advice would come in handy.

Dan leaned back and his red and white checked shirt showed under his coat as his eyes lit up at another memory. He told of a coil in a tractor that had become dislodged. The coil held the clutch in place and Dan was trying to put it where it belonged. The heavy steel spring was resistant to pull, and could only be stretched a little. Dan had the idea that if something small was placed between each coil, he would be able to stretch the stubborn steel.

What better to use than pennies! They were the right size and shape, and were available in the right quantities too. Painstakingly, Dan had placed penny after penny in the coils, moving on to another when he had stretched a ring to its max, and the unyielding steel slowly lengthened. Eventually he was able to clasp the hook into the latch.

"You just have to bend the coil when you're finished and the pennies tumble out," he grinned again, and his blue eyes crinkled half shut as he finished the story.

Mark had followed the explanation fully, and made a note to use that knowledge if he ever needed to stretch stiff coils. Were there any more tips for using the penny on equipment?

Dan, who seemed to have the gift that keeps on giving, produced another chronicle.

"Once a hydraulic line blew in a machine at the farm, and it was letting out too much oil. We wanted to restrict the flow, and not having a washer of the right size, I drilled a hole in a penny and fitted it across the line. It worked perfectly and we never replaced it with another washer."

It seems stopping flows with pennies, be it water or oil, were Dan's pet uses of the little coin.

"Isn't it illegal to tamper with currency?" Mark felt sure that it was.

"Oh yes, now I know it is illegal, and I would not encourage anyone to destroy the coins." Dan laughed. "Nor should anyone place pennies on rail tracks so the train can flatten them."

Copper felt exhilarated to be a penny. The little coin may not be necessary to trade, but it was still desirable for its shape and size, and that was good.

Penny Facts

1. The pennies used in the locomotive each weighed 2.5 grams, with a diameter of 19.1 mm and thickness of 1.45 mm.

2. The highest number of pennies produced in any year was in 2006, with a total of one billion, two hundred and sixty one million, eight hundred and eighty three thousand (1,261,883,000) pennies.

3. It cost the government about $11 million last year (2011) to supply pennies to the economy.

Penny Fun

- Play heads or tails by spinning pennies on the table to pass time while waiting for your order at a restaurant.

little copper pennies

- Place a penny on your forehead without tilting your head back and time how long you can keep it there. Compete with someone.

CHAPTER 5

AROUND THE HOUSE

The morning was cool with the crisp, spring air. Shaking the crumbs left from the breakfast toast, Olga wiped the table and rearranged the place mats in equidistant parallels. Setting the vase in the centre, she noticed the tulips were no longer standing straight as they were last night when she picked them up from the flower section of the supermarket.

The woman caressed the perfect curve of a soft, pink petal with her forefinger. Like lots of people, she connected with her plants.

"Feeling droopy this morning? I've got something for you."

Reaching for a tin can in the kitchen cupboard, Olga dipped in and brought out a handful of coins. They were mainly pennies punctuated with the odd nickels, and Copper was among them. Dropping back the nickels, she examined the remaining coins. The copper component of the penny was also a mineral in fertilizers, and Olga was a firm believer that a copper coin revived wilting tulips.

However, only a date check could confirm which penny was right. Would Copper meet the standard? Switching on the light on the stove, Olga narrowed her eyes as she tried to decipher the date engraved on the small coins through her bifocals. Her short hair was streaked with salt and pepper strands. An austere woman of German descent, she was slender and tall, and her good figure was largely credited to genetics. Olga was likeable until crossed. Always ready with an opinion on any subject, neighbours described her as a good friend or a bad enemy.

This morning there was no evidence of haste as Olga studied the coins with attention to detail that would have made a school master proud. Three were bypassed before one was found. Up to 1996, the penny was made of copper. After that, zinc and steel replaced the core metal, with only a thin copper veneer on the surface. It was imperative that a true copper coin be found.

Lucky for Copper, it was minted in the correct time frame, and as Olga slipped it in, the penny sank to the bottom of the lead crystal vase with a clink.

"There, you'll be straight soon enough." She crooned to the brilliants bulbs with their curved, green stems and touched the pink petals again.

Noticing how dirty most of the other pennies looked, she exclaimed.

"Look like you could use a cleaning!"

Striding to the bottom shelf of the pantry, she pulled out a plastic bottle labelled 'Pure White Vinegar' in black letters. Dousing most of the contents into a bowl, the woman added some salt and mixed the concoction vigorously. Bending the money tin, a stream of coins flowed into the bowl.

"Dang!" Olga's annoyance came through as some liquid splattered.

little copper pennies

Ripping a sheet of Bounty paper towel, she mopped the counter and her blouse at the same time, then washed the vinegar off her hands. With a spoon, she rearranged the coins until all were submerged in the acid juice. Like magic, the tarnished coins changed to brilliant brown. Clean as a new pin.

As she took in the transformation, Olga's face creased into a smile. Whatever the thought, it softened the harsh lines of her face and made her look pretty. Olga had drifted into a secret world, the summer when her son Lucas had turned five.

"Mommy, look. Did it fall from heaven?" The child's eyes sparkled as he surveyed the back yard. Yesterday's plain, green grass was abundant with pennies glistening with morning dew. Brushing the hair from his eyes, Lucas sped barefoot through the patio door and hopped on to the damp grass. In a flash, the little boy in red pajamas patterned with prints of Superman, his television hero, dove in and grabbed fistfuls of cold, wet pennies.

Laughing behind him, his parents brought an empty Tim Horton's coffee can to lay the treasures. David stooped down and helped his son pick up the loot that he and his wife had tossed out the night before. Olga had taken some photos. They had anticipated that Lucas would be delighted to find the pennies that appeared magically on his birthday, but the ecstasy on the child's face was beyond what they had thought. It took so little to delight a child, and the pennies had never failed to bring joy.

That year they had taught Lucas to count and group the pennies, as reinforcement to learning numbers. The little family had painstakingly made penny towers, placing the coins in columns and trying to balance them to see how tall a column could be made. Life had been good until

David's accident. Then the daily grind was harsh, much worse than the northern winters that came each year without fail.

Why did bad things happen to good people? Somewhere in an inexact time zone, Olga had ceased to trust. Lonely nights, short lived relationships and scrimping, slowly hardened her and eroded a piece of her soul. Unbidden. Unasked.

Without permission, the heart that beat in her chest had started to beat to an alien tune.

A tune of cynicism.

Then there was her kitten. Docile and contented, Jelly was black with grey stripes that were metallic silvery in their sheen. This was Olga's favourite childhood pet; better than a doll because he was real. Curled up on his cushion, Jelly stretched his soft paws in front of him. He stayed for a long time in this position, and the little girl would stop to pat each tiny paw several times a day.

Rubbing her fingers over the velvety fur, she thought that the round, little surfaces looked like the perfect place to put something small, so resourceful Olga had carefully placed pennies on her pet's feet.

"Keep this for me, Jelly."

Large, green eyes had stared back solemnly at the child, and she felt certain the feline understood the request to guard what had been entrusted. At first Jelly had smelt, and then licked the pennies. They did not smell nor taste like fish, so he promptly shook them off. Undaunted, Olga persisted in placing the coins, and by the end of the day, the furry creature acquiesced his surrender. For years Jelly would keep pennies on his paws for his beloved little mistress.

little copper pennies

Olga brushed an involuntary tear. Her rental contract did not allow cats and she had not had any for years now. Many days she did not care for a lot of things, but today she did as she gazed at the transformed pennies.

The phone ringing jolted her back to reality. She grabbed it and her side of the conversation comprised five words: "Hello, Yes, Yes, 10 o'clock."

In clipped tones more severe than she intended, Olga had confirmed to do something at 10:00 a.m. Back she went to rinse the heap of coins, and then laid them on a towel which she patted dry with the Bounty. The beautiful currency looked like a treasure from Ali Baba's cave.

Half an hour later, her friend Marie walked in with a caramel cake. The two women sat down at the table with the vase of flowers, in front of cups of hot, black tea. The warmed up cake with brown, sticky caramel, left gooey remains on the plates. When Marie commented on the lovely tulips, Olga described their droopiness and pointed to Copper lying at the bottom of the vase, finishing her story with, "They'll be straight soon."

Marie, who had not known of the penny remedy for tulips, was full of 'Oohs'. Copper was delighted to be the source of the great expectation.

"I got some new sheer drapes for my living room," Marie changed the subject. "I want to go light for the next few months."

"What colour?" Olga enquired. Her own drapes were lemon, and pleated, like those in a Sears catalogue.

"Plum. I like them, but they stick out at the bottom." Marie glanced in the direction of her purse, as the ring on her cell phone indicated the arrival of a text message. She would check it later.

"What do you mean they stick out?" Olga picked a crumb from her yellow jersey shirt. The cap sleeves showed two-toned skin on firm muscles, but Olga never bothered with tanning salons anymore.

"The hems are not staying flat. I'd like the sides to remain in a straight line and not curl at the bottom." Marie opened her napkin and demonstrated to Olga.

"So put pennies in the hem, that'll get them straight." Olga spoke as if this was common knowledge.

"Pennies?" Marie repeated the words, the implication lost on her.

In her forties, she was younger than Olga, and had come to depend on the older woman's wisdom. Her easy going nature was the perfect complement to the 'crab apple' as Olga was referred to by neighbours when out of earshot.

"That's easy to fix, pennies in the hem of the drapes will weigh them down and keep them smooth." Olga glanced at the clock after her matter-of-fact explanation. "Look, I have some pennies there. I just cleaned them and I can show you how to do it," she offered her friend.

The ever trusting Marie gratefully accepted. Another special use for pennies based on their combined weight. Copper was thrilled to learn that its friends were put to unique uses as it was in the vase.

Comfortable in its wet repose, Copper recalled a time when it had not been appreciated because of its weight. Truthfully, the abundance of pennies quickly became heavy, and there were seven more pennies with Copper that day. Before Ralph had slipped his wallet in his winter jacket's pocket, he dumped the contents and sorted what he wanted.

little copper pennies

"Stupid pennies," he fumed, "always a nuisance and cluttering up the other money."

Copper and the rest were shoved in a drawer with pencils, pins and old batteries, and shut out of sight, until one day Ralph's nephew rescued them and they came back into circulation.

Copper was called a nuisance. Scorned and rejected because of weight and supply, it was music to the little coin to hear that pennies were desired because of their weight, to keep the drapery hem hanging straight.

"Do you want to fix the hems now?" Olga's question was more of a suggestion.

Marie nodded. Olga scooped up some of the newly cleaned pennies and the pair headed out of the door. At the same time a deep, cheerful voice was heard outside.

"Nice day, Olga, Marie." It was her next door neighbour, Keith Poppick, holding a trowel in his hand, and smiling from ear to ear in a chirpy manner.

"Yeah, what's up?" Olga called back and paused for a quick chat. Keith explained that he had been removing the lino from the bathroom and was trying to put in tiles.

"Big job, huh?" Olga commented. Keith laughed self-consciously.

An expert as a computer programmer, he had stated before that he was not very handy around the house. Keith sometimes uploaded photos for Olga which she picked up at Walmart, and whoever got the snow blower out first, cleared the two driveways.

"I had to do some tiles over because they were crooked," Keith commented a bit sheepishly.

"What about the plastic spacers?" Olga brushed a cobweb from the wood siding of her house as she asked her question.

"The hardware was out of them, so I didn't get any." Keith picked up a bottle that a passerby had tossed over his fence. Didn't people know that they shouldn't throw bottles on other folk's property?

"Use pennies then. You get a perfect edge if you put them on all sides." Another matter-of-fact response from practical Olga. Then she added, "I'll come over and show you," and called to Marie that she needed a moment.

Penny hunt on the grass, penny in tulips, kittens keeping pennies, pennies in drapery hems, pennies to space tiles....Learning that pennies could be used in so many novel ways was a proud moment for Copper. It wanted to be a great ambassador, but its expectations were exceeded. Falling value or not, pennies were needed and little Copper felt wonderful.

Penny Fact

1. The last copper penny was produced in 1996 with 98% copper, after that pennies were copper plated.
2. It costs 1.6 cents to produce each penny.
3. If adjusted for inflation, an 1870 penny would be worth about 31 cents today.

Penny Fun

- Set up a penny hunt for children by tossing them on the grass or hiding them in different places.
- Roll a penny down a hard, smooth floor to see how far it can go.

CHAPTER 6

THE COLLECTION AND A BIKER

Dropping, dropping, dropping, dropping
Hear the pennies fall.
Every one for Jesus,
He shall have them all.

Ruth trilled the little chorus she had sung in Sunday School nearly three decades ago. Soon after logging on to Facebook, she had exclaimed in surprise, "The penny is going to be eliminated?"

Clicking on the link, the brunette read the article's headline: *Mint will stop making pennies this fall.*[1] She was quiet as she ingested the news, the look on her face one of shock. Her dark curls hung around her head in soft coils as she gazed at the computer screen.

Quickly she messaged back, stating her response aloud as she typed. "Many learnt of missions through the penny. Sad to see it go for that reason." Her white, French tipped finger nails clicked on the keyboard as she pressed the letters.

Walking to the microwave where two pennies lay on top, the thirty-two year old woman picked one up and blew off the dust. It was Copper and its year said 1959.

"Missions." she repeated to herself. Copper knew exactly what she meant.

Having been placed in many offering collections over the years, Copper had been counted, rolled, and sent to the bank with other pennies, innumerable times. Then the little coin was given back to other customers. Over and over the cycle was repeated. As it changed hands through trade, Copper saw many places, partook in events and was privy to conversations that could melt ice.

Ruth's little song was an old one. Years ago, children used to sing the catchy tune, *Dropping Pennies,* when they were putting offering into the bag, and adults used to join in deeper voices. Come to think of it, neither Ruth nor Copper had heard the song lately.

The jingle of coins bouncing each other was a wonderful sound that always brought smiles to the children's little faces. At one church, a medium-aged boy named Darren, with dimples on his cheeks, used to snap his pennies into the burgundy collection bag, so it could produce the loudest sound. Some children would giggle and others seemed to burn the action in memory as if to try it out. Still others look scared as adults frowned at them to be silent. Copper did not mind being snapped for entertainment.

At another church, flat, white boxes shaped like drums, with red lettering and crosses, were given to each child. Once the box was assembled, a slot at the top allows the pennies to be dropped in. The mandate - Save your pennies and bring it to help the poor. That children's class was buying a goat for an orphanage in Africa.

little copper pennies

There were many Sunday School teachers, but Ruth remembered one lady with a lovely smile, and a yellow dress. With long, golden hair parted on the side, she looked like the angel figurine in the foyer of the church. This teacher told the children the most amazing story of a little coin's value. It was about a widow who put two small copper coins in the offering. That day, Jesus was sitting in the temple near the treasury, the place where the people placed their offering.

The angel lady had talked about a mixed crowd at the temple. The rich ones dressed in fine clothes made of expensive fabrics were putting in lots of money. Then a woman, not well dressed at all, because she was very poor and had very little money, came and dropped in two copper coins.

The teacher related how Jesus called his disciples and showed them the woman.

"This widow has given more than anyone else here today," Jesus told them and they looked at him as if to say "Yeah, right!" Then Jesus had explained, "The others gave money but still had lots remaining. This woman gave all the money she owned."

The blonde Sunday School teacher had smiled and said that small sacrifices of poor people meant more to God than the lavish donations of the wealthy. The little coins like Copper proved a point that the heart of the giver is more important than the size of their gift.

Copper felt like a hero. It was proud to be a one cent piece. It was a really good feeling to know that a copper coin was in the Bible, and is used to inspire people up to the present. Talk about penny power!

Collecting pennies has never gone out of fashion. Penny drives are not unique to churches, as a lot of schools fundraise with them as do clubs, communities and just about anyone wanting to make a difference in the lives of the less fortunate.

Ruth had received a giant baby bottle as a gift when she was born and she talked about it many times.

The oversized bottle resembled a baby feeding bottle. It was clear and the cap was a large, white and pink, plastic nipple, with a slot for coins. For many years Ruthie, as she was called then, piled pennies into the bottle. It took forever to get full but finally it was. With her mother's help, her six-year old fingers had placed penny after penny into paper rolls. Painstakingly she filled and rolled, and filled and rolled again. Three times they had trekked to the store for more wrappers, only to find that they were out of stock on the last trip.

"I can put them in Ziploc bags." Ruthie rushed in the direction of the kitchen in earnestness, her long dark curls swinging up and down.

"The bank will not take plastic bags, sweetie," her mom explained to the child, "I'll get some rolls when I go to the city."

Soon the day came when they stood before the teller in the bank.

"How can I help you?" The teller asked her mom.

"It's her that needs help." Her mother gestured to Ruthie on the left, who was barely discernible behind the tall counter. They were both holding the heavy bags of metal currency.

little copper pennies

The teller leaned forward to see the child and commented on how cute she was with her crisp, dark curls and big, luminous eyes.

A teller at the next station, who had no clients then, came over to look at Ruthie. Gauging from their reactions, it did not look like diminutive customers made frequent appearances at the bank to conduct their own business.

"What can I do for you?" the woman gently asked Ruthie.

The little girl stuttered back, "I want to change my pennies."

Ruthie and her mom heaved the bags on to the counter. Counting the dollars aloud, the teller handed it to the child.

"Eighteen dollars for you," she chimed, "what are you going to do with all that money?"

"Eighteen dollars?" Ruthie repeated the words as a question, and her already large eyes grew even larger. Like liquid pools of the bronze she had just exchanged, her brown eyes sparkled as she touched the dollars with tenderness akin to reverence. This was her money.

It was another poignant moment for Copper: the unified value of pennies.

Coins that some think have no value.

Coins that were sometimes tossed into jars among buttons, paperclips, rubber bands and anything that had no specific home.

Coins that were thrown unceremoniously on the nearest surface available, often forgotten and ignored. Considered a nuisance and described as inconvenient, worthless and heavy.

"I will buy Easter eggs for the seniors' home." Even as Ruthie replied, she held tightly on to the bills, as if afraid they could get lost.

The child's little kindness had delighted the seniors, and many of them had patted her cheeks and hugged her. Dressed in blue tulle and chiffon, she floated like a fairy princess as she offered her basket of eggs to staff and residents at the home.

Savings like hers bought gifts for children living with their mothers in domestic abuse shelters. Pennies like Copper bought clothes and toys for children in orphanages. A penny helped someone get food. Copper had seen people's tears, their struggles, and their happiness. The little coin had been to many provinces, and had been owned by person of status and persons living in poverty.

Like the woman with the straggly hair that hung on the side of her worn face. Her mouth was droopy and her back was slightly stooped. She moved slowly and paused for breath after every second step. Pork and beans had been her meals for the last week, but she was grateful she could afford that. There were no more Social Insurance cheques. There was also no heat in the house as the furnace was broken.

Limping to the aisle with canned foods, she reached for the familiar tin with its picture of brown beans nestling in the thick sauce. She was so hungry she could have eaten the picture. Her gaze lingered on the soups next to it, but there was no decision here. The soup will only be one meal. The beans could spread over three meals if she spread it thinly on the stale bread she was rationing. Picking up the beans, the forlorn woman went to the checkout counter.

little copper pennies

"Eighty eight cents, ma'am." She fumbled with the tattered purse and handed the cashier of the variety store some coins. He counted it.

"You're six cents short," he barked. Another quick fumble and she passed over the one nickel that remained.

"You owe me a penny." He was irritated.

Looking at his chin, the woman murmured, "I don't have any more money." The attendant barely heard her but the empty purse spoke loud and clear.

"Sorry." His tone was clipped and the can of beans vanished under the counter as he shoved her money, one cent short of the total, back at her. He was not really a mean man, but if the cash till did not balance, then the difference came out of his earnings. Too many customers showed up with pennies short. This man knew that a penny here and a penny there added up, and on minimum wage, that was a lot to deduct.

Tears of shame had filled the woman's eyes. She hunched down even lower as if the stares of the other customers in the line pierced her back.

Then a gruff voice broke the tension, "Here's a penny."

A muscular biker with a tattooed arm slapped a brown cent down and the purchase was complete. Whispering a broken 'thank you', the woman accepted the proffered beans that resurrected from under the counter, and shuffled out of the store. Her benefactor looked a bit intimidating, with his head tied in a red bandana and bushy eyebrows half covering his eyes, but it was clear to all that his heart was kind.

Mostly, Copper saw the value of one cent.

Removing the physical penny coin would affect low-income families and poor people the most as they tend to use cash most. Those people do not seem to mind the inconvenience and time needed to roll pennies and take them to the bank. When pennies are no longer distributed, prices will be rounded down or up. Since the poorer people usually make smaller purchases more often, they will experience rounding up more often and hence have to pay more.

Copper was concerned that those people may not be able to afford the higher prices. When money is tight, every red cent counts. So children, poor people and those without cards, will shoulder most of that burden of eliminating pennies.

Little copper coins have always made a difference. They pass on positive values. They teach children how to save through penny power. Though Copper is the least profitable denomination, because by itself it cannot not do much, its power comes through unity. Collectively, with other pennies, they become thousands of dollars.

Copper dared to wonder. When pennies are gone, will the giving stop? Will small charities be able to carry on their good works? Its cousin the nickel will be the next smallest denomination, but that may not be given away so easily.

Even though the little coin ponders, it accepts its fate of elimination. For it know it is a hero, and a true hero never dies.

Penny Fact

1. W.H.J. Blackmore designed the reverse of the 1911-1920 penny.
2. Canadians can still use pennies to pay for items and the one-cent piece will retain its value indefinitely.

3. The composition of the most recent penny is 94% steel, 1.5% nickel, 4.5% copper plating or copper plated zinc.

Penny Fun

- Create dumb bells for exercising by filling pennies in socks and tying the open ends. Wrap them around your ankles or wrists as weights. Longer socks work better.

- Start a hobby of collecting pennies from as many countries as possible. Storing them in coin holders or coin albums is ideal.

CHAPTER 7

THE PENNY IN THE CAKE

Walter's great grandparents lived in a cave during their first winter on the Prairies in the late 1800s. Albert and Edna Lord, and their little girl, Linda, could not build a house during the harsh winter months, so a hole was carved in the earth and the little family stayed warm until the spring of the following year when a small house was constructed.

Walter did not recall hearing of complaints either. Eager to start a new life, the emigrating family took life in stride and met the daily challenges with practicality and resourcefulness.

Money was scarce and the penny was valuable then. Receiving one was a treat, and little Linda had obtained a coin in a way that is still familiar to many…

Here's seventy nine cents for you." The cashier in the tiny bank identified each new piece to Edna Lord. "Three 20-cents coins, one 10-cent piece, one 5-cent and four pennies."

"Thank you." Edna held out her hand and accepted the money. She ran her fingers lovingly over the currency and tucked them in her purse. The pennies back then were larger than the present day penny, closer to the size of the modern 25 cent piece. The one-cent piece of 1858 is also no longer in circulation.

Walking out of the bank, she gazed again at the spotless coins, turning them over in her hands. Placing the others carefully back in her purse, she lingered over the bright penny. The golden ball of July sun against the blue sky was mirrored in both its round bronze face, and the periwinkle blouse that was neatly tucked into her voluminous skirt with its checkered print. Edna placed the money gently in her bag, and shut it out of the scorching sun.

The bronze coin piece desired above everything else in its special kind of heart to be a good ambassador for its beloved Canada. It would be patriotic. It possessed value.

Edna started off for home and on arriving, hurriedly unhitched the horse from the wagon. Leading him to a dented metal trough, she called to the little girl peeping from the window.

"Hello Lindy, we'll get started on the cake soon." Her British accent was charming, and as she spoke, the small face disappeared from the window.

The child's real name was Linda and her birthday had passed two weeks ago. Edna had promised her little daughter something special when she returned from the town that day. She was going to maintain a tradition she had brought from her native country. Taking out her purse, Edna sifted through the coins and took the penny out. Ever so gently she laid it out of sight on the mantelpiece.

Seven year old Linda's blue eyes shone as brightly as the coins. Soft curls waved around her pink cheeks when she moved. Linda was moving a lot, fetching a wire whisk, which gleamed in the light from the open window, and a clean, wooden bowl which she set on the little table with its white flannel cloth.

The girl helped with the eggs while her mother worked on butter and sugar. Then Edna mixed in the remaining ingredients: flour, water, baking soda and maple syrup, along with some vanilla essence from a little bottle. The maple syrup had been gathered from the trees whose leaves were embossed on the penny's reverse side. The coin was excited on its high seat on the mantel.

"Can I taste it, Mother?" Linda pointed to the mixture clinging on to the sides of the bowl. She could hardly wait for the next hour while the cake baked in the fireplace.

"Yes, it's all yours, dear." Edna smiled into the delighted face of her child, who was wasting no time in scraping the bowl with her fingers. As she scraped, she licked the sweet paste.

"Yummy." she said and went for more. Occupied with scraping and licking, Linda did not notice her mother reach for Copper and after a quick wash down, wiped it and wrapped it in wax paper. Turning the cake pan to where the sides joined, she set the coin carefully in the batter and it was hidden. How delightful! The fireplace was no way as hot as the London mint, but the penny was glad to feel that temperature again.

While the coin baked in its sweet, moist home, white clouds sailed in the country sky and a cool breeze rustled the thin curtains. Linda changed into her best dress, blue and white flowered gingham that matched her azure eyes. Huge sleeves puffed on each arm, and a white sash tied around her tiny waist, was gathered in a neat bow at the back. Black shoes, and white socks that matched the apron, peeped when she walked. Her golden hair was pulled back with a band made of the same blue fabric of her dress.

Soon it was time for the cake to be taken out of the oven.

"It's very hot, Mother," Linda drew back as smoke escaped from the cake. Edna nodded, making a little mark with a knife at the spot where the cake touched the joining at the sides of the pan.

"It will be cool soon and Father will be coming in." Edna assured the excited child. An hour later the cake was placed on a plate, and spreading a thin layer of white icing on the top and sides, Edna again made a mark near where the penny lay.

A rumbling sound outside sent the eager girl to the window. "Father's here." Linda screamed in delight.

"Be careful with your dress." Her mother's admonition as the child raced for the door was gentle. The medium built man with dark hair and a genial smile, lifted the girl and spun her around the room.

Albert hastened to wash his grubby hands and they settled for dinner. Linda could hardly eat, and finally the trio gathered around the beautiful, white cake, one parent on either side of their offspring. Albert's deep voice led the chorus, as he had done for all the years that Linda could remember:

> Happy birthday to you, happy birthday to you,
> Happy birthday to Lindy, happy birthday to you.

The small coin had never heard this song before, and thought it was a most beautiful one.

"Now you must cut a slice this big, Lindy," and Edna indicated to the right and left of where the penny lay hidden. Then it all made sense. Edna had used the joint in the tin pan to track where the penny was. Could it be that the little coin was Linda's special present? A penny, with its one-cent value?

The penny was silent in its hiding spot as Edna scooped the slice into a smaller plate with a chipped edge. Then she served pieces to her husband and herself.

"The birthday girl must taste hers first," Albert urged in his strong voice, though Linda needed no encouragement. With the side of her fork she cut a piece and placed it into her waiting mouth.

"Ummm," she exclaimed, nodding her head. "It is good." Linda stuck her fork in again and a dull thud sounded as she struck the penny wrapped in waxed paper.

"What's this, Mother?" The child looked in surprise at the ingredient that was clearly not edible. Taking the coin between her small fingers, she removed the paper wrapping. The penny was as shiny and new as when it had left the bank.

"Ooh." A gasp slipped out of her cake-filled mouth. "It's a penny."

The parents smiled at each other over the head of the surprised girl. "See, the Queen's portrait is on one side and a wreath of maple leaves on the other side." While her dad explained, he took the coin in his hands, roughened by hard work, and touched its face, turning it over and reading its inscriptions aloud.

He gave the coin back to Linda who traced its edges with her finger, the desire for cake gone in the discovery that the penny belonged to her. Then Edna explained to the child that in medieval times, people of England used to place coins in the batter of the cake. Anyone who found a coin was believed to live a good life, become wealthy and get married.

"This is worth a lot, Lindy," the farmer assured his small daughter, "You can buy bread, sweets, pencils, and other things with it."

"An ice cream cone too," piped in Edna.

"Thank you, Mother and Father." The girl took turns hugging her parents. "I will not lose it. I will put it under my pillow when I go to sleep tonight."

The little copper penny was needed. It had a purpose. Next week Linda would take it to the store and the coin would find new adventures. For now, it was a new friend, greatly loved by a child who in the dark of night, checked to be sure that her birthday penny was there.

Penny Facts

1. In 1858 the one cent, 5 cents, 20 cents and 50 cents coins were minted in England as there were no minting facilities in Canada yet.

2. The one cent piece was round, with diameter of 25.4 mm, and made of 95% copper with a minimal alloy of 4% tin and 1% zinc. The image of Queen Victoria, the Queen of Canada, with a laurel wreath in her hair was embossed on one side, and the reverse featured a wreath with maple leaves on a vine, and the words ONE CENT 1858.

3. The design of the maple leaves wrapped around a vine on the 1-cent coin of 1858-1911 is the work of L.C. Wyon of the Royal Mint.

little copper pennies

Penny Fun

- Ask someone much older than you what a penny used to buy. Compare the items to current pricing.

- To make round corners on a photo or scrapbook item, use a penny to trace a curve line then cut it with scissors.

CHAPTER 8

THE OLE DAYS

Wilma's voice quavered as she reached back into the 1920s when she was a little girl. Cash was scarce and a cent as she preferred to call the little coin, purchased real things. She was correct about her preference. Copper was in fact a cent, a word that came from the Latin *centum* which means one hundred.[1] A cent was one hundredth part of a dollar. In Canadian French, the penny is also called a *cent* which is spelt the same way as the French word for 'hundred.'

Penny is really a slang word for the pence, the currency of the British imperial system that was previously used in Canada. People, however, in Canada and the United States use the terms penny and cent interchangeably.

Wilma, who was born in a farming family, was telling her experiences to Michaela, a plain faced, brown eyed girl with two, long braids on either side of her freckled cheeks. Since the news broke that the penny was being eliminated, children were given homework to ask their grandparents and other older persons what a penny used to buy.

"Mama would sell a dozen eggs for 10 cents." Wilma seemed flattered by the interest of the keen Michaela. Even if you're not good at math, it is easy to figure out that back in those days, one egg cost less than a penny. No kidding about value.

Though Copper was not the penny that paid for the eggs, it wished that it was. Right now Copper sat in a clear, glass bottle with other coins and a few marbles, feeling mighty proud of its old penny friends from the last century.

"We never left a cent on the ground," the storyteller admonished the girl, wagging her forefinger as she spoke. "Oh no, if one fell, we looked for it and when we found it, we kept it safe." The old woman shook her grey head for emphasis.

In this present time, most people would not bother to look for Copper if it was dropped. With its lowering value, no longer able to buy an egg or anything else, many think it is a waste of time to go after the little coin.

At ninety years old, Wilma's posture was upright and her memory sharp. She wore her short hair like a cap around her head, and dimples on her cheeks merged with the wrinkles when she laughed. Hazel eyes that were still bright, pierced her face, like a bird fully aware of its surroundings. Wilma was quite nimble for her age.

"With two cents, some people could buy a pound of potatoes. My family did not buy potatoes as we grew them ourselves," Wilma continued. Nor did they buy meat. Their cattle provided meat, milk, cheese and butter.

"But some people used to buy a briny bone or salt meat for a cent to make soup." Michaela looked surprised and the old lady informed further. "Mama did our baking, so we did not buy baked goods, but some people would buy a cracked piecrust for a cent."

That was certainly penny power, and Copper felt pleased.

Then Wilma described the animals they raised and how much she loved the little calves and piglets. They were her friends on the farm, and they would nuzzle against her legs when she went to feed them. She would pause from her chores to run her hands on their backs, and to rub their heads. With a small pitch fork, the little girl used to spread hay for the calves to lie on.

Then she chuckled as she remembered, "They liked it when I would scatter a forkful of straw on their heads."

She recalled her dad selling pork for six cents a pound in the 1930s, and beef for twelve cents a pound. It was very expensive to ship cattle when they were sold, and the buyer would have to pay for the animal freight ahead of time. This could cost anywhere from $30.00 to $35.00.

Wilma did not get money often and she related how rich she felt when she was given a penny. She got one for her birthday in the cake and for Christmas, and when they went to town. Sometimes her relatives gave her pennies on occasions too. Copper felt sad that the girl Wilma did not have much money, but oh, so happy that when she got a penny, it was her treasure.

She was already grown up when she first saw the penny vending machines that spilled out handfuls of salty peanuts and candy pieces. As she talked about the old fashion register next to the counter on which the vending machines stood side by side, Wilma beamed at the recollection. It was as if they were calling her name to catch up and taste the morsels she did not buy during her childhood. Jellybeans, red hots, mojos.

Larger piece treats that were also sold for a penny included licorice, bubble gum, peppermint stick, lollipops, peanut brittles and jaw breakers.

"The jawbreakers were wonderful and they hurt my cheeks," she recalls. "Mama bought three jawbreakers for a cent. I loved them."

Aptly named because the hard candy could not be bitten or chewed, jawbreakers remain the most popular memory of the value of a penny by the older generations. The layers of sugar of the large, solid, colourful balls could only be dissolved by sucking. Wilma easily spent an afternoon of delight on these treats, and if she was careful, they could be spread over days.

Though Wilma sucked a lot of jaw breakers she did not get a variety of other tasty sweets that the one cent bought. Luckily, her cousin Shirley, whose family was fairly well off, used to bring samples of the much desired confection that Wilma's little heart craved to taste. Red and white peppermint striped like a clown's trousers. Scrumptious peanut brittles shaped like the shell in which the nut grew. Buttery toffee and nutty caramel wrapped in waxed paper. They were all coveted pleasures that accompanied Shirley's visit from the city.

"I didn't ask my parents to buy different candies because money was so scarce," the old lady said. "I was happy with what I got."

It looked like Wilma was a contented little girl. Not just contented, but mature too. She understood hard times and hard work, which was reflected in her independence and agility as she entered another decade. Looking at her, it was easy to imagine her as a girl with straight dark hair and a heart shaped face in which hazel eyes danced green or brown, or sometimes both colours. Her hands were small and slim now, so it must have been that way when she was little, shovelling straw in the barn.

Wilma's chair slid back and forth. It was a newer version of a rocking chair, with flat legs that moved in grooves instead of the curved legs of the type she grew up with. She did not care for those anymore, as they moved out of place and touched the wall when she rocked.

The senior lady was narrating how at the carnival, Shirley had bought popcorn for a cent, and had eaten a whole caramel apple, which cost three cents at that time. Shirley had also gone on a ride on the Merry-Go-Round, and on a pony, each for a cent. Wow, there had been so much value in a penny in those years.

The newspapers were sold for three pennies each. Wilma's family did not read a lot, so they hardly bought it, but when she remembered one being bought, it was read line by line, page by page, from front to back. Several times over. The three-penny paper was not tossed out as trash, and there was no recycling in those years.

After all the news had been read and reread, the paper was used to wrap gifts, especially the comic pages. They also made paper jets for play, and laid pages on the floor as a mat. What that little coin bought, and how cleverly its products were used, was fascinating to hear.

"You could buy a postcard for a cent," Wilma was saying pensively, "but most times I made my own cards because I liked to draw."

The old lady had been on a roll from tale to tale, and Michaela had been very quiet and had not interrupted. Now she interjected, "I like making my own cards too," and the two smiled at something they had in common. "And I never had a pony ride, but I went on the Ferris wheel when the amusement park came to the city for the Exhibition."

Rides at the amusement park now cost many dollars. Copper's worth had really dropped to the point where there was no purchasing power in this century, and it had become more of a nuisance than a help.

Here Wilma got up and walked to the adjoining kitchen from which she brought a plate of Rice Krispies squares. Michaela eagerly thanked her for a square, and as she munched her hostess continued: "Some children traded bottle caps for a cent, but I never had any to trade." The woman laughed and her fingers formed a circle as if she was holding the prized token. "Some of them used to play pitch games but I used to only watch."

Her voice dropped and Michaela dabbed her eyes vicariously for the loss young Wilma must have felt as she watched others have fun, but from which she was excluded. Games she could not play because she had no pennies. Hers was a hard life, and even though one cent more here and there could have given her a lot of extra happiness, she had been deprived. Still, she was contented.

Michaela bowed her head as if she was in a holy moment. In some ways it was, or so Copper thought. Most of the stories were new to the girl and it was remarkable that Wilma never complained about what she lacked. What was sorrowful was that it was obvious that more pennies could have added to her joy.

It was poignant to hear about Copper's one time cent value. Though worthless now, it was once prized, and a little girl longed for some pennies but was too poor to own much of the coins. All the same, it was the kind of memories that made the little penny feel good on the eve of its passing.

little copper pennies

Penny Facts

1. After Queen Victoria's reign ended in 1901, King Edward VII began his reign and his portrait was used on the penny from 1902-1910.
2. From 1911 until the end of his reign in 1936, King George V portrait was used on the penny.
3. A Canadian penny roll holds 50 pennies.

Penny Fun

- Place a penny on the back of your hand. As fast as you can, drop your hand downward, and at the same try to catch the penny in the palm of your hand.
- Use a penny as a bookmark.

CHAPTER 9

MORE OF THE GOOD OLE DAYS

Isabelle touched Copper in the pocket of her thin cardigan. She carried the penny around because it reminded her of all the pennies that once had value to buy a single item. Then she took Copper out and set it on the table of the coffee shop, drinking in the details of Bill's anecdotes more than she did the hot chocolate in the white ceramic mug. She loved hearing the stories from the good ole days when a penny had its own power to buy items.

Bill is a natural storyteller. At six feet two inches, he jokes about being the second shortest male in his family, grinning as he sketches the others who tower an additional five inches. His large frame is encased in blue jeans and navy Helly Hensen jacket, which he informs, is made from recycled milk jugs, plastic ones. The letters HH were printed neatly in white letters on the left side.

Isabelle's expression was ecstatic as Bill told of the years that were shared to him as stories. His parents had grown up during the Depression of the 1930s and money was very scarce. Back then, instead of buying items at stores, bartered goods and traded services were the exchange. In fact, stores were very scarce, almost non-existent in the struggling towns of the Canadian Prairies.

The old man's blue eyes dimmed as he remembered his parents. His dad was a Swedish/Scottish farmer, and his mother had 'a bit of every nationality, including some Cree.'

"Dad said in the 1940s he used to buy a cigarette for a penny in the cigarette machine," he recalls. "I never saw a machine but he would put a penny in the slot and a cigarette would pop out."

Then his eyes brightened and a smile broke on his clean shaven face, as he rehashed his own years, when, with his twin brother John, the young teens had earned pennies. This was in 1957.

"John and I used to sell rides for a penny on our little horse, Poika," he chuckles at the memory. He described the dapple grey gelding, Poika, as good natured and willing to do anything, except pull a car. To overcome this resistance, the boys would place blinders on the animal, and with only tunnel vision, the horse was tricked to move the car in tow.

Poika was traded to another family over some winters so he could ride the small children to school, as their little legs could not make the long walk in the snow. No cash was exchanged.

Bill told Isabelle of the weekends, when the lads took Poika to the baseball diamond and sold rides to kids, ranging in ages from toddlers to ten years. For one cent, a child would ride on Poika's back, from home plate around the bases. This was a big event, and the energetic teens, possessing both the charm and tongue of the keen marketer, drew customers in large numbers. Often children took multiple rides, and Bill reported with pride that one weekend, the brothers had earned over twelve dollars.

"That was over twelve hundred rides," he announced. "All we did was give rides for days."

This was really great news. A penny for a ride! It was wonderful to remember the value Copper's one cent once possessed. As it faces retirement next winter, in many ways it was like the little coin was hearing its eulogy.

Bill explained that with the earnings, the boys bought Christmas presents for their parents and siblings. The cash flow from less profitable weekends was used to support the newly acquired fondness for cigarettes. He was quick to add the disclaimer, "That was the only time I did cigarettes, and oh, I bought penny matches in the little cards."

Penny matches. Another star for little Copper's value.

"We got three jawbreakers for a penny." Bill paused, as if he was savouring the sugary taste of the round treat. He sips his coffee and adds, "Six more when a pop bottled was returned to the store."

In his day, a deposit of two pennies was made on a bottle of pop. When the glass bottle was returned, the two cents would be refunded, but Bill often chose six jawbreakers instead. "Yes, I could happily spend a whole afternoon with jawbreakers," he soliloquizes. "The same with the bubble gum we got for a penny. The Hubba Bubba gum. Those made the largest bubble you could ever want. It could cover your face and if it popped on your eyebrows, then that could be something to remove."

He also described the comic strip paper that was wrapped around the bubble gum, with characters like Spiderman. Bill had built a collection of comics for a while.

With both the jaw breaker and bubble gum, he could suck or chew until his jaws ached.

Isabelle rubbed her finger on Copper's circular outline as she listened.

Bill grinned again. "The tooth fairy always left a penny for us."

Which child has not willingly endured the pain of a loose tooth to gain the coveted penny? Still laughing he adds, "My granddaughter now demands a loonie for her tooth."

Since Copper has been in circulation, it had been placed under pillows a few times. Oh, it was so much fun to hear the children squeal when their tooth was gone and a penny was left instead. Working with the tooth fairy was a delightful task as an ambassador. Nowadays, greedy children demand more money for their tooth, but however high the price rises, the legend will always be 'a penny for your tooth.'

Isabelle was asking about when payment was short. A few years ago, many stores started carrying penny dishes, where customers could take a penny if they need one, or leave one if they did not need their change. She was curious as to what was done in the past. If a child did not have a penny in the 1950s, did the storekeeper withhold the purchase?

Bill shook his head. "Actually, I could charge a penny to Mom and Dad's account." His eyes veered slightly to the right of the coffee shop as a customer opened the fridge to take a pop. Then he continued, "The storekeeper would write it on a charge account he kept on a foolscap sheet of paper, and my parents would pay it when they went to the store."

Copper's value was accounted for. It meant something and was not dismissed.

Then Bill talked about the penny fundraiser at school. He got a card that was divided into 100 small squares. A penny was placed in each spot and when full, it amounted to one dollar. It was a wonderful way to raise money.

The senior man had another great memory. "We could get ten minutes of parking time for a penny at the parking metres in Manitoba."

Ten minutes of parking. Wow. In that era, it was probably the same in many parts of this great nation. In our present time, ten minutes of parking would cost twenty five cents in rural areas, and higher in cities. Copper was happy because the little penny had truly been a winner.

Here Bill drained the last of his cold coffee as he came to an end of the exciting narratives. The faraway look in his eyes was gone and the approaching night signalled that Isabelle should go too. How many other celebrations of the penny were there?

Unknown.

What Copper's special heart knew was that it and its little penny peers, soon to be taken out of circulation, would be fondly remembered by the old, and leave dents in many hearts.

Penny Fact

1. The 1936 dot cent, which has a tiny dot below the date, indicates that this is a 1936 coin produced in 1937. There are only three known specimens of the dot cent, and in January 2010, one was auctioned in New York City for over $400,000.

2. The two maple leaves design on the 1920-1936 penny was created by Fred Lewis and coincided with a reduction in diameter to 19.05 mm.

3. King George VI portrait was used on the penny from 1937- 1952.

Penny Fun

- Play penny triangles. Place three pennies in a triangle and flick them with your thumb and forefinger. Always keeping the pennies in a triangle, flick one penny in a straight line between the other two without hitting either pennies.

- Use pennies to create different shapes and figures by stacking them together or placing them side by side.

1858 Canadian penny

The 1858 penny was slightly larger than a present day quarter. More pennies were produced in 1859 before production ceased. The technical specifications remained the same until production resumed.

<u>1858 to 1875</u>

Composition: 95% copper, 4% tin, 1% zinc
Weight (g): 4.54
Diameter (mm): 25.4
Thickness (mm): n/a

1876 penny

Production of the penny resumed in 1876. The coin was slightly larger than the present day quarter and maintained its technical specifications up to 1920.

1876 to 1920

Composition: 95.5% copper, 3% tin, 1.5% zinc
Weight (g): 5.67
Diameter (mm): 25.4
Thickness (mm): n/a

1920 penny

In 1920 the penny was reduced in diameter to the size we know today and at the same time adorned with a two-maple leaf design. The technical specifications remained the same until 1941.

<u>1920 to 1941</u>

Composition: 95.5% copper, 3% tin, 1.5% zinc
Weight (g): 3.24
Diameter (mm): 19.05
Thickness (mm): 1.65

1936 dot cent

The tiny dot appearing below the date denotes this as a 1936 coin made in 1937. There are only three known specimens of this coin, with this particular example being sold in auction at New York City in January 2010 for over $400,000. The technical specifications are the same as the 1920 penny.

1937 penny

In 1937 the famous maple leaf design by noted English artist George Edward Kruger Gray made its appearance. The design features two maple leaves on a twig, and has appeared for the highest number of years including the present, changed only for short periods to commemorate special occasions. The technical specifications are the same as the 1920 penny.

1942 penny

This version was unchanged from 1937 other than increasing the copper content by 2.5%. The technical specifications remained in effect from 1942-1977.

1942 to 1977

Composition: 98% copper, 0.5% tin, 1.5% zinc
Weight (g): 3.24
Diameter (mm): 19.05
Thickness (mm): 1.65

1967 penny

Canadian artist Alex Colville created this Rock Dove art for the penny as part of a special Centennial package incorporating Canadian wildlife on the various denominations. The technical specifications are the same as the 1942 penny.

1978 penny

The composition was changed slightly by increasing the tin content and reducing the zinc. The technical specifications lasted until 1979.

1978 to 1979

Composition: 98% copper, 1.75% tin, 0.25% zinc
Weight (g): 3.24
Diameter (mm): 19.05
Thickness (mm): 1.52

1980 penny

In 1980 the size of the penny was changed for the first time since 1920. The diameter was reduced by .05mm and a slight reduction in thickness resulted in a weight saving of .44 g. The technical specifications were in effect until 1981.

<u>1980 to 1981</u>

Composition: 98% copper, 1.75% tin, 0.25% zinc
Weight (g): 2.8
Diameter (mm): 19
Thickness (mm): 1.45

1982 penny

In 1982 the penny adopted a 12-shaped side to help the visually impaired distinguish it from other coins. At the same time another .3g was shaved from it weight. The technical specifications were in effect until 1996.

<u>1982 to 1996</u>

Composition: 98% copper, 1.75% tin, 0.25% zinc
Weight (g): 2.5
Diameter (mm): 19.1
Thickness (mm): 1.45

1992 penny

The 1992 penny was dated "1867-1992" as part of the Canada 125 years celebration. The technical specifications are the same as the 1982 penny.

1997 penny

The coin reverted to the round design in 1997 as the 12-sided shape was difficult to plate. The penny was also switched to a copper-plated zinc coin, reducing the weight by .25 g. The technical specifications remained the same until the present.

<u>1997 to present</u>

Composition: 98.4% zinc, 1.6% copper plating
Weight (g): 2.25
Diameter (mm): 19.05
Thickness (mm): 1.45

2000 to present penny

The 2000 version of the penny replaced the copper-plated zinc core with a steel-nickel core, resulting in a .1 g increase in weight. Since 2000, the 1-cent coin can be produced using either the copper-plated zinc of 1998, or copper-plated steel compositions.

<u>2000 to date</u>

Composition: 94% steel, 1.5% nickel, 4.5% copper plating
Weight (g): 2.35
Diameter (mm): 19.05
Thickness (mm): 1.45

2002 penny

The 2002 penny was dated "1952-2002" on the portrait side to commemorate Queen Elizabeth II's Golden Jubilee. As a result, this coin appears at first glance to be undated. The technical specifications are the same as the 2000 penny.

2012 penny

The final penny was produced on May 4, 2012. The technical specifications are the same the 2000 penny.

2000 to 2012

Composition: 94% steel, 1.5% nickel, 4.5% copper plating
Weight (g): 2.35
Diameter (mm): 19.05
Thickness (mm): 1.45

CHANGES IN THE METALLIC COMPOSITION OF THE PENNY

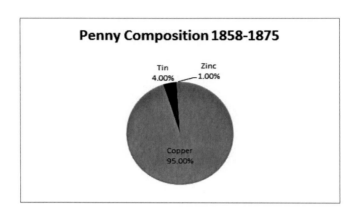

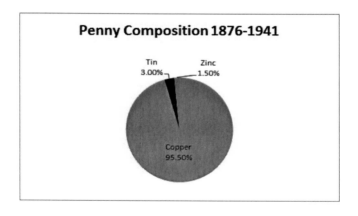

little copper pennies

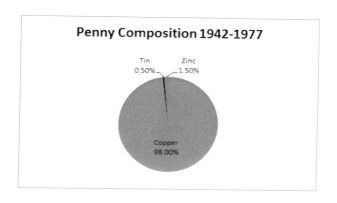

Penny Composition 1942-1977

Tin
0.50%

Zinc
1.50%

Copper
98.00%

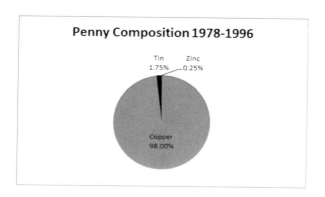

Penny Composition 1978-1996

Tin
1.75%

Zinc
0.25%

Copper
98.00%

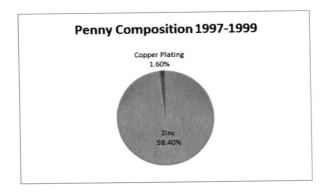

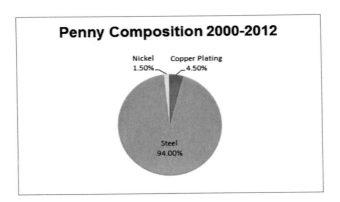

*Note: Since 2000, the 1-cent coin can be produced using either the copper-plated steel or copper-plated zinc compositions. *Source: Royal Canadian Mint.*

CHAPTER 10

GRADE FIVE

"Attention, boys and girls." Miss Cartier called the fifth grade pupils to order. The class before lunch was noisy, due in part to hunger pangs inciting restlessness in the stomachs of their little masters, but mostly to the arm wrestling antics of Tate and Cory. Cheers and shouts from the audience in the middle of the room drowned out her directive. In one corner, a group of girls was applying lip gloss. Another group was huddled over a cell phone, an item banned during class time. Only a few children seemed to notice Miss Cartier had arrived.

"Tate, Cory, cut it out." The teacher of French descent walked briskly towards the young boys. A look sent the spectators skulking to their seats, and magically Social Studies binders appeared on tables. The girls scampered to their assigned spots and propriety was restored. The children liked the pleasant teacher with her silver rimmed glasses and silver speckled hair. She often regaled them with stories of her native Quebec, though she was quite contented out west.

In one hand Miss Cartier held a newspaper and in the other, a see through bag from which she took Copper out.

"Ella, could you pass one out to each person?" The teacher handed the bag to the tall, slender girl, who had been sitting attentively since the period started.

"What's in there?" asked Ethan, who was sitting in the second to last row at the back. He could not contain his curiosity. His tousled brown hair and freckled nose and forehead gave him an impish appearance, and some of his escapades made adults wonder if he was not related to another world.

Rachel, who had already been served the contents of the bag, informed the class loudly. "It's a penny."

Giggles erupted. Someone spun theirs and it clinked to the floor.

"A penny? What for?" Skylar wanted to know. Most teachers did not bring pennies to class. Even on days when hot lunches were sold, loonies and toonies were the requested coins.

Miss Cartier held up the newspaper with bold headlines and read: *"Pinch Penny - Canada's copper coin to go".* At the same time, she lifted Copper in view of the class. Some of the pupils looked at their pennies too.

"Where's the copper coin going?" Though Ethan sounded cheeky, his question stemmed from a genuine desire to understand the perplexing headline.

"Maybe to jail." More giggles erupted at Skylar's response. Her recently glossed lips parted to show white teeth as she smiled. Visions of iron bars danced before Copper, and though those are to be shunned generally, it may have been a better outcome.

"Actually, it could be worse than jail," Miss Cartier joined the humour. "Who knows what's happening to the penny?"

little copper pennies

Ella's hand was in the air again, revealing rows of coloured elastic bands on her slim wrist. The teacher smiled at the girl who had helped distribute the pennies. A disciplined pupil who showed interest in things around her, Ella seemed the kind of girl who would set goals and accomplish them.

"There won't be any more pennies made after this year." Ella replied, her chair scraping the floor as she sat down.

"That's true; my mom read it in the papers." Tate's wavy head bobbed up and down as he stated his consensus.

"Ohhh." An audible gasp went through the class and eyes opened wide. Many students picked up their pennies as if burning it in memory, as they tried to comprehend the information.

A chorus of "Why?" sounded. Without waiting for answers, everyone started to speak. Questions like "What will we buy things with?" and "I have a lot of pennies in my piggy bank. What will happen to them?" were thrown at no one in particular.

"One at a time, please." Miss Cartier beamed at the interest the subject was generating. "Why do you think the penny is being removed?" she asked.

"I think it's something like it cost more to make the penny, but I don't know how much." Though absorbed in shading the penny with his pencil, Tate contributed to the discussion.

That was correct. It actually costs 1.06 cents to make the little one-cent piece, and it was only worth 1.00 cent. Having been introduced to decimals and rounding off, the children understood the numbers in concept, if not quite in reality. The price of metals used to make pennies, copper, zinc and steel, were rising, making it unprofitable to keep producing the little coins.

Like other government businesses, the mint is expected to be financially responsible, and producing something with a value less than its manufacturing cost, is not very good financial sense. On the green board, the chalk squeaked as Miss Cartier wrote the explanation in neat lettering, and the pupils copied it.

Ella raised her hand again, and at the nod of her teacher, added, "My dad says the penny is worthless and can't buy anything."

Barely were the words out when Skylar interrupted. "That's not true. I have lots of pennies and I buy candy and bubble gum at Mr. Tam's." She was referring to the little Pop shop that kindly Mr. Tam ran two doors from the school. Call it crazy but Copper felt good to be defended.

"And when I took my pennies to the bank and got $5.00, I went to see *The Chipmunks*." Cory chirped triumphantly. "My grandma said it's a good way to save and she helps me collect pennies."

Many heads nodded as if this was true of them also.

Pennies are really a good way to save, there was no discounting that. At the same time, pennies are also seen as a waste of time because they take up a lot of space in pockets and purses, and are heavy. Miss Cartier nodded and wrote on the board again.

"My mom teaches my little brother to count with pennies," said Rachel, "so the penny is important. Miss Cartier, I don't want the penny to go."

"Yeah, me too." The echo of pre-teen voices was a wonderful sound. Clearly this group adored pennies.

little copper pennies

Copper felt special. If the little coin had had wings it would fly over the country and peep into schools where thousands of similar debates might be occurring.

"Can I keep this penny?" Cory wanted to know. More voices added their pleas.

"I love pennies." Skylar was cradling the little coin in her palm. It was quite clear that children would miss pennies when they were gone. They are a group that pick up pennies and use them for games and education.

"Yes, you can keep your penny or give it back if you don't want it." Miss Cartier smiled and placed Copper back in the bag as the jarring of the school bell announced it was time for lunch.

Penny Fact

1. One hundred pennies make up a 'loonie' the Canadian one dollar coin, and the two dollar Canadian coin is given the slang name 'toonie'.

2. The round coin with the maple leaf twig is the most popular penny design, having been used since 1937-1966, 1968-1981 and 1997-2012.

3. Since 1908, the Canadian mint has produced 35 billion pennies, half of them in the last twenty years.

Penny Fun

- Place a penny on a flat surface and cover it with a piece of paper. Using a blunt pencil, shade it up to the circular edge. The details of the penny transfer to the paper. Repeat on the other side on a new piece of paper.

- Toss pennies into an empty can or jar. The person

throwing the most pennies into the can wins all of them.

CHAPTER 11

HIGH SCHOOL DEBATE

Sunlight streamed through the large rectangular panes of the west wing of the high school, making the day look warmer than the minus 8 degrees the thermometer attached on the outside showed.

Inside the classroom, hearts with arrows, initials, and odd calculations decorated the desktops. These normally stood in rows of two, but today the fourteen students were haphazardly huddled in a group. Some were perched or leaning on desks while others sat on chairs. In the centre was a desk with an 18 inch laptop.

On the white screen, a table was drawn with two columns, titled PROS and CONS in bold letters. A heading at the top of the document identified the subject of the debate in red letters in font 16, *Removing the Penny*.

Meghan, a blonde girl with an ostrich feather weaved into her hair, was typing notes, and Julie, petite and possessing Type A personality, was leading the discussion on the removal of the penny from the coin circulation. The students had to present group reports for course work in Economics, but thought it best to have a preliminary discussion. Copper lay near the hinge of the laptop, just under the brand logo, *Acer*.

"The penny is part of the currency system and all coins have value." Brian a serious faced young man was articulating. "One penny as a unit might be uneconomic, but collectively, there's value. Penny drives for charities are neat examples."

His contribution was carefully transcribed by Meghan.

"And, if you remove the penny, prices will go up and stuff will cost more." Jenna spoke while she popped a red M&M into her mouth, and offered the bag to Raj who was sitting next to her. Higher prices usually implied inflation and this was flagged appropriately under the Cons.

"Don't be so sure," Raj contradicted as he dipped his hand into the proffered bag. "New Zealand, Australia, Sweden and some of those other countries that abolished the penny, did not have inflation."

Some students nodded. It was true that many nations abroad had completely abolished their denominations of least value, with almost no impact on commerce. Nor did consumer confidence wane in the monetary system. In 1989, New Zealand had gotten rid of its one penny and two penny coins without hiccups. Then in 2006, the country eliminated its nickel.[1] Copper remembered when those decisions had escalated its own nightmare of being removed.

Chewing on the sweet candy, Raj continued, "In 1992, Australia removed its one-cent and two-cent coins, and Sweden has removed many of its coins about three different times."

Everyone, except Meghan who was summarizing on the keyboard, was staring at Raj with a kind of look that said

little copper pennies

"weirdo" or some equally fond description of a peer who remembers things that the rest cannot recall ever hearing. Stocky built and muscular, Raj was an avid reader on international affairs, the kind who might also be a solid Minister of Finance in the future.

To be exact, Sweden had removed its one-öre and two-öre coins in 1971, and by 1992, it had also removed its five, ten and twenty-five öre coins. In 2009, the fifty-öre coin went.[2] Australia had progressively eliminated its most minor denominations, the one-cent and two-cent pieces from circulation after a mere twenty six years of its being.[3] The coins went down under, literally.

It appeared that all of these changes in different economies around the world had occurred without significant problems. Those citizens did not seem to lose faith in the currency system or their leaders' decision. On the contrary, it can be claimed that once the currency was stable, there was little, if any, negative effect on revamping the coin supply. Canada's currency was undoubtedly stable. Even if there is inflation, it would be minimal.

Now Lin was speaking, "I still think prices will increase. I read that prices will be rounded up or down. No sweat if it's down, but anything that goes up could bring inflation. Let's do the math." Lin grabbed a binder, not his, and yanked out a page. Brian handed over a pencil from a nearby pencil case.

A visual learner, Lin scribbled numbers while he talked. "Let's say there are one million transactions a day that is rounded up by two cents, that's two million cents more that customers have paid. The only way this could cancel out is if you round down the same number of transactions by two cents. But," he paused, "a consumer really don't know if the transaction will be rounded down. It will be an honour system, but who's checking?" (See Appendix 1 for an actual exercise with 100 transactions.)

Someone yelled, "Go dude."

Jenna attested with "Good point Lin," and touched his shoulder in acknowledgement of his common sense.

From the side, Pierre, a blond guy with blue eyes, aimed a friendly paper ball at Lin, who promptly tossed it back. "Bet you will check and report to the government," was his observation.

Lin's concern was something to consider. It had been reported that business would be expected to apply their rounding in a fair and transparent manner, but with no official watchdog over this, it's anybody's guess that fairness will occur.

"Don't forget the penny is still legal tender." Tripp was saying and the keyboard clicked as Meghan's fingers with it red nails created words on the backlit screen. As a unit of measurement, the little coin would remain unchanged, but as a physical presence, it will be phased out come next February.

Julie was urging the others for more points and the topic of debit and credit cards came up. Most of the young men and women had cards, though the majority were debit cards.

"I have a credit card that's tied of my dad's account," explained Kazi in slightly accented tone, "but he checks my limit." Kazi's family owned an optometry business in the city.

"Sweet!" Jenna grinned, "Wish my dad would do that." Long blond hair hung down her back, and bangs covered one eye, giving her a cute, pirate-like appearance. Jenna actually got gifts of credit cards that were bought over the counter and which were activated by a code at the register. This she used for purchasing things online.

Jillian, a tall girl of seventeen in the back row, volunteered, "I have a debit card, but I take out cash first and then buy my things with cash."

Copper felt needed. Snacks, cinema tickets, burger meals, and costume jewellery were among the cash uses for this group. The removal of the penny may not affect credit and debit card transactions, but these young adults were not yet credit worthy. Babysitting jobs, cutting lawns and casual work at restaurants did not approve them for credit cards. A cash generation still existed, until a steady and more substantial job was acquired. Copper felt good to be in demand still.

The laptop shifted as Meghan stretched, and the little coin slid in between the hinge.

"It's not like I carry around a lot of pennies," Nicole was saying. "They are heavy but I always like to have a few. I think the penny's kinda cool."

Call it silly but Copper found it nice to be called 'cool.'

"Yeah, and you can get even with it too. Just drop a cold one down someone's shirt." Jenna giggled at her own joke. In good humour, Meghan inserted a third column, and labelling it 'Pranks,' she typed, 'drop pennies down Jenna's shirt.'

Raj pulled the debate back to focus. "I think when the penny is stopped, nickels will take over. There will be an increase in demand for the metal nickel …"

"Except the 5-cent piece is now made of steel," interrupted Brian. He looked even more serious than before. "The nickel could one day face the same problem as the penny, with cost of production being higher than its purchasing power."

Jenna reached across the desk and hi-fived Brian who blushed fiery red, and voices chorused their "uh huhs." Then Raj drew some cost curves on his page and the youths talked energetically back and forth. These kids were on top of their economics.

"What about going green?" Kazi offered softly. "I heard on the news that some 7,000 tonnes of pennies were manufactured over the last five years. When the penny is gone, the government could recycle, save on metal, and storage and distribution costs."

Meghan typed the points furiously. She already had three pages of tabled information. A private sector study had estimated that the economic costs of maintaining the penny, including direct production costs and indirect costs to financial institutions, retailers and consumers, amounted to $150 million in 2006.[4]

The young people were saying that it would be hard to see the little coins go. A part of history was being erased, and there still was a lot of sentimentality about the penny, especially from female groups.

The school day was drawing to a close, and as there were no other ideas, Julie wound up the group study, and Copper was pulled from its crevice as Meghan closed the laptop.

Penny Fact

1. In 1953 to the present, Queen Elizabeth II's portrait has appeared on the penny, though she started her reign in 1952.
2. The Canadian Currency Act states: "A payment in

coins … is a legal tender for no more than … 25 cents if the denomination is one cent." (Section 8, 2e).[5]

3. The last Canadian penny was minted on May 4th, and distribution of the penny will cease on February 4, 2013.

Penny Fun

- How many words can you find with 'penny' in them?
- Check your penny jars for older coins and start a collection with at least one penny from each year.

CHAPTER 12

THE RETAILERS MEETING

The stout hardware owner mopped droplets of perspiration from his red forehead. The room was getting hot though the air conditioner pushed cool air. To prove his point, Morris was standing and pulling an overstuffed wallet from his pocket. Emptying the contents of one compartment, a few silver coins jingled on the table.

"There, only silver. No need for pennies." Morris sat down again, breathing heavily.

Not to be outdone, Karen fumbled in her black leather bag and pulled out a handful of money. As the others watched, she placed them in front of her. Copper tumbled out along with an assortment of nickels, quarters, loonies and more pennies. "Customers want exact change when they make a purchase," her voice was calm. "You can't make proper change on a cash transaction if the penny is gone."

The five people in the room, retailers of small businesses in a rural town in Saskatchewan, had been asked to provide feedback to the Town Council on the perceived implications on business if the penny was removed. The entrepreneurs had met in small groups as their schedules permitted.

A man who appeared to be in his early thirties was scrolling through a Blackberry. Tall and well-built, his brown hair was cut low, and the open collar of his white golf shirt flashed a gold chain.

The lady next to him was older and elegantly dressed in a blue pant suit with which she wore a lime-green shirt. She operated the local pharmacy and her name was Jean. Her dark hair hung in a short, blunt cut that framed her pleasant face and suited her cheerful disposition. Copper had sat in her till many times, handed as change to customers then given back again as payment. Actually, the little coin had been in each person's till at some time or the other.

"It might be easier to handle cash without pennies in general," Jean was reasoning, "it reduces the counting, wrapping and handling. And I could use the extra space in the till."

Morris nodded his agreement. Then Michael, the owner of the Blackberry spoke up. "I'm for faster service and no more pennies to roll." He did not look up but continued pressing buttons on the handheld. Michael operated the small car dealership, tire shop and bus depot in the town.

"Customers will complain when the price is rounded up." This came from Amanda's low voice. She ran the beauty parlour and an attached variety store.

Amanda had the most beautiful appearance. Her short blond hair spiked upwards and sideways, and the spikes were frosted in shades of black and turquoise. Deep, black liner circled her blue eyes which were framed by the longest black lashes a girl could want. They did not

little copper pennies

look real, but it was attractive on her tanned, smooth face. Amanda looked as if she was eighteen, but as she had been in business a few years now, she was definitely older.

The talk was that businesses will have to apply rounding to cash transactions to remove the need for pennies. At the convenience store, people had been vocal in stating their liking and need for the penny to Karen. Copper felt good about being needed.

"Rounding will not be done on every single item, only on the total bill of sale." Morris clarified in a more mollified tone.

"And that total includes all the taxes." Again Michael didn't lift his head, but no one seemed to mind his multi-tasking.

"I've heard customers say that they think business owners will round up prices to make more profit." Amanda contributed, "They don't believe that we will round down prices."

She was referring to the government's guideline for rounding off prices that involved pennies.

Prices ending in one or two would be rounded down to 0. If it ended in three or four, it would be rounded up to 5.

Prices ending in six or seven get rounded down to 5, and rounded up to 0 if it ends in eight or nine.

Morris shifted in his chair and it squeaked. "As long as I don't have to change prices on the shelf, they can scrap the penny next week." More beads of perspiration appeared on his bald head.

Copper felt hurt to be dismissed so casually. Morris viewed it as useless. He wanted the little coin gone because it was a bother. Call it crazy but Copper wanted to stay. Even if it was taken to the bank years after sitting on a shelf, the penny would be happy. The little coin craved to remain in Canadian heritage.

Placing her Snapple bottle down, Jean inquired. "Wouldn't we have to change all of our prices if there were no pennies?"

"It's more complex that just re-pricing goods." Michael actually looked up from his Blackberry briefly as he spoke. "It's the accounting for taxes and balancing tills at the end of day. And think about it, cash registers may have to be reprogrammed. That's pricey. Software and upgrades cost a lot."

The others wrinkled their foreheads as they absorbed this information. It looked like most of them had not thought about the tax aspect. It was looking like getting rid of the penny would be more of a nightmare for them than the two cents inconvenience their customers would endure. This change entailed confusing processes, a lot of work, and unpopularity. Not just with customers but with staff as well. Its population aging, Canada still embraced a lot of seniors in the workplace, and many of them were downright hostile to what they saw as electronic interferences.

Michael was speaking. "And there could be a forced inflation when prices increase." His eyes were still glued to the mesmerizing Blackberry.

The Karen spoke, "The truth be told, we do benefit from pricing goods ending at .99, you know, that psychological aspect of $9.99 instead of $10.00."

She looked at the others meaningfully and Morris shrugged and replied, "Oh well." No one seemed to want to discuss psychological pricing further.

little copper pennies

Amanda looked in each direction to encompass her four colleagues. As she did, her large, round earrings swung and touched her cheeks. "Just to be sure, are we only talking about cash sales? Not debit and credit cards sales?"

"That's right Amanda," Jean smiled her confirmation. "The penny is physically going to be removed, but it still has value as one cent."

Seeing a look of confusion on Amanda's face, Karen quickly explained. "You can still write cheques for totals with pennies, and all electronic transactions like your credit and debit cards will not be rounded. It will be paid to the cent."

Outside, the wind chill had dropped to minus 23 degrees and sleet was hitting the ground in tiny ice pellets. A storm was not expected, but one could never be certain how the weather would change during winter in these prairie towns.

Michael stretched his legs and added. "Depending on how you do business, dissing the penny can affect you differently. Sales on my end are mainly through plastic."

"Mine's too, except for some bulk items," was Morris' addition.

"At the store if it's gas then debit and credit cards are usually used. But for munchies and cheaper things, cash is used, and especially with the children." explained Karen. Jean nodded and so did Amanda. A lot of the older people and the children used cash.

The talk shifted back to pricing. "I use a lot of pennies, but if my customers are fine with it being removed, then I have no problem." Amanda drummed manicured acrylic nails softly on the table.

Karen glanced at the clock on the beige wall that showed it was nearing lunch time.

"This topic is not exhausted but I think we could wrap up now." Jean concluded the meeting. "It looks like operationally we could have a lot of repercussions by the phasing out of the penny. But we must support our government's decision."

Almost in unison, the five were out of their chairs. Karen scooped Copper back into her warm bag.

Judging from what the little coin had heard, it did not seem as easy to get rid of its physical presence especially in the tax aspect. The penny was an ambassador and is here to serve so Copper too will support the final decision.

Businesses however, did not need to worry about updating cash registers for rounding, since prices and the final total payment will still be set at one cent increments.[1] Instead of having to grapple with rounding-off prices during the busy Christmas shopping season, banks and businesses were given a few more months in which to train staff and inform customers of the changes.[2]

Despite the reprieve, there is no hope that the little coin would live, but it was comforting to know that its signature .01 would still be present on receipts and invoices. Now if only Copper could find more way to immortalize itself!

Penny Facts

1. The 1992 penny was dated 1867-1992 as part of Canada's 125 year celebration.
2. Introduced in 2003 the latest obverse effigy on the penny depicts the Queen without a crown. The portrait was designed by Suzanna Blount.

3. After the Mint ceases distribution in February 2013, businesses will be asked to return pennies through their financial institutions to the Mint for melting and recycling of the metal content.

Penny Fun

- Measure the tread depth of your car tire by placing a penny in the tire groove with the Queen's crown facing down. If you can see the top of the Queen's crown, you need to replace your tires.[3]
- Toss a penny to settle a wager or start a game.

CHAPTER 13

D.G. AND OTHER SYMBOLIC MEANINGS

Catherine was preparing for a talk on Out Of the Box thinking. She was voicing her thoughts aloud as she recited the goal for her OOB as she called it: look at something familiar from an angle you have never thought of before. Dissect it, dig it through, mash it, do anything to come up with something novel you have not considered before.

In an effort to brainstorm unique and creative ideas, she opened the top drawer of her desk for inspiration. A Bic pen stared back at her. Idly she picked it up then dropped it in favour of the staple remover. Still uninspired, the chic executive moved the contents with manicured fingers, and the rummage revealed Copper.

Catherine picked up the penny and was about to drop it back, when she paused. Her keen eyes had caught something. Eagerly she examined the inscription on Copper's face, then turned it over and read the other side, and turned it on its face again. The little coin was curious as to what caught her attention, and did not have to wait long to find out.

"1960," she whispered through red lips, referring to the date on the penny's reverse. "We were born the same year."

This was Copper's first lesson in OOB thinking. Looking for parallels in its bronze face and her lighter one; for experiences that were mutual. She was a warm, laughing, brilliant administrator, and Copper was a cold, useless coin. The penny was interested to see how this would unfold.

Catherine talked to herself as she worked. Right now she wore an expression of someone who was on the verge of a breakthrough. That she meant business was emphasized when she shut the door of her office, hastily tacking a handwritten "Do not disturb" note on the door. Soon her pencil was sketching a herringbone map on her pad with the points:

- Significance of number one
- Significance of metals
- Significance of Dei Gratia Regina
- Significance of maple leaf
- Significance of 1960 combined numbers
- The Queen

"Drat, I only have time for three points," she was mulling. Too much information could clutter her presentation, so a swift decision saw the pencil circling the first three tenets.

The penny's reverse side has the number 1 embossed. It is a single entity. Catherine seemed convinced that outside of the numeric system, the number one represented something. Copper was intrigued about any significance, however far-fetched it may be, of the wider meaning of its value of one. Call it crazy but ONE has purpose.

"As the first child I'm number one." The pace of words uttered by the attractive woman in a royal blue power suit matched the movement of her fingers, and the large screen of her desktop with a PowerPoint slide took life as letters appeared in colour. "Number one reflects new beginnings."

So too it was with the penny; created for the new beginning of the decimal system that Canada was adopting, and for which it was minted. Catherine was summarising this parallel on the second slide.

Then there is the significance of 1 as purity. The little coin's innocence as a currency is different from most of the other coin denominations it circulates with. It is used for helpful purposes around the house, in repairs, for savings, and purchases primarily by children and the poor. Quick thinking Catherine was recording this. The pages were increasing when the phone rang, but the energized lady, focused on her work, touched a button and the voice-mail came on, politely requesting that a message be left.

Copper's low value kept it straight. It has not been used for bribes and its little amount kept it from being used for vices. No one exchanged it for cocaine and alcohol. Children were happy to find the little coin and charities thrive because of its unit worth.

Catherine was finishing the first tenet as she typed, "Number 1 is unity and purity, and penny power is most obvious when pennies come together. That's Team work in Motion."

The monitor changed and illuminated 'Google' and in a second, a website produced metal compositions. Catherine browsed it briefly, resting her right fingers against her chin as she read. A ring with an oversized cobalt stone adorned her forefinger, and her gold watch was a beautiful contrast against the rich blue fabric of her jacket. She was fashionable all right in black high heeled pumps, and earrings and necklace also in gold.

Then she was typing quickly into the slide, creating a summary from the facts she was reading. The first penny minted in 1858 was a bronze alloy of 95% copper, 4% tin and 1% zinc. The majority metal was copper.[1]

In its natural state, copper is reddish brown in colour. At that time, all coins had to be made of metal that was worth the actual value of the coin, minus a small amount to cover the cost of making them. Copper was chosen for the one cent piece, as it was inexpensive, easy to work with, and could make a right sized coin that contained a hair less than 1 cent worth of metal.

Though Catherine voiced many words, she summarized the thoughts in short bullets. With its bright, metallic lustre, copper is usually compared to the radiant sun. Shiny has been the word most often used to describe Copper and its peers as they roll out of the mint. A penny in 1960 and up to 1996 was made of 98% copper, 1.75% tin and 0.25% zinc.

Chemistry and speculative philosophy holds that the elemental alchemy symbol for copper is also the planetary symbol for Venus. As such, this symbol embodies characteristics as love, balance, feminine beauty, and artistic creativity.[2] If anyone was balanced, beautiful, and artistic, it was this accomplished lady.

The metal copper has a melting point of 1,083.4 degrees Celsius and a boiling point of 2,567 degrees Celsius.[3] At the mint, the copper is heated to 750 degrees Celsius in order to plate the penny.

The penny has been referred to over and over as the workhorse of the money system. It's quite an honour to be given that title, actually. The little coin's value is less than zero in purchasing power, but its significance lies in the historical connotation.

The pioneers of this wonderful land, Canada, placed all their eggs, so to speak, in the basket of the horse. Not only was the four-legged creature a primary mode of transport across the undeveloped terrain, it was the sole equipment in agriculture. Pulling ploughs, hauling harvested crops and moving heavy wagons were the horse's duties.

Catherine's family owned a farm and she had ridden many horses. She understood that Copper was not compared to a recreation horse. A grassroots workhorse is its symbolism. In recognition of having performed faithfully under heavy and prolonged use, Copper was proud to be termed a workhorse. Like the horse, the little penny was dependable, enduring the toughest conditions of trade and work.

Workhorses had to be strong or they lost their place and value. In 1998, the little coin's core was changed to a composition of 98.4% zinc, with 1.6% copper plating on the outside to maintain its brilliance. Zinc with its melting point of 419.58 degrees Celsius and its bluish colour, was not to be the penny's primary for long. Symbolically, you could say it was not as enduring as a workhorse.

So it is not really a surprise that the little coin became the strongest it could ever be, literally, in the year 2000. Its new body was made of steel; 94% steel, 1.5% nickel and my 4.5% copper plating. The eye could not discern that Copper was any different, not even with its fraction of a gram increase in weight.

Catherine murmured as she typed. Steel reflected the penny's falling value and nil purchasing power, and that reminder is always a bit tough for the little coin to swallow.

Yet, faithful ambassadorship has been its aim, and proudly Copper can declare that it was the strongest physically than it had ever been. Or would ever be.

For steel is a symbol of strength and a workhorse must be strong, and for Canadian commerce, the little penny was strong.

Here Catherine paused and flexed her neck. To the right and then to the left, upwards and downwards. Reaching for a bottle of Aquafina water, she swallowed half of its content, and refreshed, set out to address her third and final tenet.

Another Google search for the strange words DEI GRATIA REGINA proved that it was a Latin phrase. Gazing at the monitor, without warning, the executive stopped on a swift intake of breath. Placing her left hand at the side of her head, she leaned back in her chair and stared up at the white ceiling of the office.

Only she wasn't seeing it.

Nothing lay above her office except open skies, and Heaven. The place from where the Grace of God flowed, for the words DEI GRATIA REGINA means 'By the Grace of God, Queen.'

The 1960 penny had the Grace of God inscribed in Latin. All the other coins had them too, but Catherine had never in her half century of living, wondered about those foreign words. Now she was transfixed. There was no need for further research, as the rest would be written from her journey of grace.

Delving into her black, leather bag lying in the bottom drawer of her desk, the brunette's groomed hair fell forward as she raked the bag for something. Coins they turned out to be, of all denominations. One by one, through new and puzzled eyes, she read each and sorted them into two piles. One pile had one coin, the other had eleven.

In haste she turned to the untiring internet, and scrolling on the Royal Mint's website, she gave an "Aha" of triumph as she read these words aloud:

1965 - Maturing Monarch. A new obverse sculpted by Arnold Machin portrays a more mature Elizabeth II, wearing a jewelled tiara. The legend, too, was revised: the formal Dei Gratia was reduced to D.G.[4]

The eleven coins Catherine had placed in one pile had the initials D.G., and naively, she had thought that those were the initials of a person. She had not attributed it to an abbreviation of Latin words. It was not a far-fetched notion, as KG on Copper's reverse was indeed the initials of the artist George Edward Kruger Gray, who had designed the maple twigs. The little coin wondered if most people thought like that. This change took place over 47 years ago, and the younger generation may have overlooked it as well.

The Windows screen saver, flashing a hypnotizing show of colours and edifices, had obliterated the slides, but with AutoSave doing its job, Catherine had no need for the computer just then. Her whirring brain would capture it better in pencil and paper and then she'd summarize it on the PowerPoint.

She possessed a strong faith and in verbalizing her thoughts, Copper learnt a most unique discourse about how the woman viewed a penny. They were her personal thoughts but the little coin wondered if others shared the views. To her, God's name is holy even on a coin, and it should not be used in vain. Neither should it be stepped on.

Catherine shuddered. She dropped pennies carelessly and never bothered about their worth. Above all, she would never pick up a penny from the ground, unless if it was in her own house or car. Now she felt a twinge that she had desecrated God's name and His message of grace because of her disdain of the penny. The word 'Grace' means 'unmerited favour.' It cannot be earned. It was freely given and she had trampled on it. Literally.

Catherine bowed her head as she soliloquised about the penny, with her office door shut. Symbolically she had shut her heart in ignorance, but now it was opened. D.G. was like an affirmation that she lived each day because of God's grace. Over the years, the mint had produced thirty five billion pennies, which she chose to view as 35 billion reminders of God's grace raining over this huge land, blessing the entities that used the coins.

Yet it is written not only on the penny but on every coin, the sum total of which was too overwhelming to even imagine. She had never given thought to the symbols and engravings on the penny, but now enlightened, Catherine could not go back to her previous oblivion. Like most people who experience a paradigm shift, her behaviour was changing.

Every penny reassured her of her relationship with God and His favour. Catherine declared that she will never let a penny's message be wasted again. Her personal mission would now include the unthinkable act of picking up pennies. For picking up pennies is a tangible reminder of God's goodness to her and she was thankful for it. Picking up a coin is an acknowledgement of God's blessings that she so did not deserve.

Catherine's OOB exercise was sobering. When she shared it later that week, she would not be expecting anyone to adopt her mission, but change driven by passion, always ignites respect. This was her personal OOB success. She would never scorn little coins again.

She would pick up any penny, appreciate any penny, not to become wealthy but to become richer. Richer by the grace of God.

Penny Fact

1. In 1911, King George V began his reign and the phrase *Dei Gratia* (means By the Grace of God) was removed from the penny. The 1911 pennies became known as the Godless coins.[5]

2. The words were added back in 1912 due to criticism by the public.

3. In 1965 the formal DEI GRATIA was reduced to D.G., under the reign of Queen Elizabeth II.

Penny Fun

- Use pennies to replace missing tokens in board games.
- Use pennies to scratch tickets, PIN numbers and codes in documents.

CHAPTER 14

PICKING UP PENNIES

The kangaroo pocket of Sarah's old sweat shirt was slightly ripped. Blowing her nose in an already used tissue, she stuffed it back into the pocket and continued walking to school. She was passing the park when Copper fell out. The gooey tissue took up much of the space and the little coin slid through the hole and landed on some soft sand. Sarah kept on walking, not aware that the penny had fallen. She would be unhappy when she found out that she could not buy a bag of chips because it was missing.

Questions danced before Copper like Northern lights on a clear night. How long will it be here? Will someone rescue it? What if it's never picked up?

The unaccustomed feel of gritty sand was not pleasant, but Copper could not move. Call it diva but waiting was longer than the little coin thought it would be.

Footsteps approached and Copper's hope rose. Surely its new, bright coat would attract the passerby. As quickly as its expectation soared, it was dashed. A shadow fell and a heavy cross runner descended on the penny's flat face. With a rough nudge, Copper was sent spinning into another heap of sand and landed near a bench.

The little coin felt cross. It was now out of sight from the main path, and the possibility of someone finding it looked dim. So did the rayless light of the sun. The wind was picking up and trees began swaying in the cool air. Copper hoped Sarah's cold would not be worsened by the change in weather.

Suddenly large drops of cold water pelted down in the April morning. It was not long before the penny was baptized in the puddle that had collected around it. The hours wore on and evening approached. Still no one came near it. Night fell, and then came the next day, and the next.

Copper's brilliance was fading and it was beginning to look unattractive. This made the little coin feel worthless and it shivered several times. Not because of low temperatures, but more so due to the pain of loneliness which waned its optimism as the days passed. Did anyone care?

About a week later, on a warm evening, two women strolled by.

"I need a rest, Gina, there's a bench," one of them said and they turned in Copper's direction. Finally, the penny had some company. As they took their seats, the bench moved and creaked slightly. Copper wondered if these women knew Sarah.

"Your lace is undone Eileen," Gina observed. Eileen bent forward and with deft strokes, the lace was retied. As she straightened up, she spied Copper and bending again, plucked the little coin out of the dried mud that had been its bed for over a week.

"A penny," she said rubbing the sand off on her grey sweatpants.

little copper pennies

"For heaven's sake, Eileen, it's a dirty old penny." Gina wrinkled her nose in distaste.

Copper lay quietly between Eileen's fingers, surprised, yet not surprised at her friend's words. What would Eileen say?

"Not much dirtier than the ones people pull out from their shoes," was the swift rejoinder. "Or the change you get at the shops. Have you thought of how many people use the toilet and don't wash their hands, then grab some money to pay for their stuff? Or cough in their hands then pick a penny from the "take a penny, leave a penny" dish? I'd rather touch dirt than people's germs."

"But it's a worthless penny," Gina stubbornly held on to her view. "And besides, wouldn't you be embarrassed if someone sees you picking up a penny?"

"What's there to be embarrassed about?" Eileen eye-balled Gina as if she suspected she was being judged.

"Well, you should leave it for people who really need it." Gina was looking at the trees in the distance. The small green buds would soon transform the bare boughs to a healthy mass of leaves. On the street to the left, a car crossed the intersection, and then it was quiet again.

"Are you asking me if it might look like I'm desperate for cash?" Eileen's laughter startled a chickadee on the nearby willow, and it flew off its woody perch.

"Gina, a penny is not worthless," Eileen was using a tone usually reserved for children. "They add up to dollars. And they're lying all over parking lots, and pavements, and streets, tarnished like this one." She held Copper out to her friend. "But it you clean it, you'll see that nothing's wrong with it."

Eileen paused and pulled a cigarette from her pocket, then fumbled for a lighter.

"The problem with us Canadians," she continued, "and maybe it's around the world too, is that we don't think that wealth is made up of small change. If you think of a penny singly, it could be insignificant. But each one has value and together they have power. Penny power is what my father called it. He taught me that I should always pick up a penny. He did it all his life and I do it too."

Lighting the cigarette, she put it to her lips and puffed out a ball of smoke which disappeared in the balmy evening air.

The two lapsed into a silent reverie as Eileen ended her impromptu lesson to Gina, all the time rolling Copper absentmindedly with her forefinger and thumb. The little coin felt good to have someone stand up for it. It did not like the mud and water in which it had laid for a week, so it could not blame anyone else who felt a muddy penny was to be shunned. However, it was really nice to be wanted, and since many persons now carried hand sanitizer around, it is possible to pick up a penny and then clean their fingers.

"I don't think it's worth my time to pick up a penny," Gina remarked. This was a crushing statement to Copper.

The worst moment of the little coin's life is when it is dropped and not picked up.

When it is passed over in scorn.

When it is tossed because it is seen as lacking in value. Copper's special kind of heart felt grieved at Gina's words.

Eileen was shaking her head. "Have you ever needed a penny and not had one? Not all stores carry a change dish. That's only a recent thing. Ninety nine cents wouldn't cut it for an item priced at one dollar. Oh no, you need that penny." She spoke with the voice of wisdom and experience.

"I have way too many coins in jars at home, collecting dust. I could barely lift them; they're so heavy." Gina waved her slim hand for emphasis. "The banks would not take pennies unless you wrap it in a coin roll, and it takes a lot of time to roll. Not to mention, it's another hassle to find wrappers." She scuffed the sand idly with the toe of her white tennis shoe.

"Big deal, then get the kids involved. Ask the neighbour's children to help. They'll do it. Then give them the cash when you change it at the bank. Kids and teenagers always need money." Eileen spoke with the authority of one who had done this several times. Inhaling on her cigarette again, she blew it out.

Tossing the ash with a movement of her fingers, the self-appointed instructor became philosophical. "You know the saying, 'a penny saved …'"

"Is a penny earned." Gina finished the maxim.

"And it's more than that," Eileen interjected. "You pay taxes on a penny earned, but none on the one you pick up."

Copper thought it was a really smart point. They used to talk about taxes when it was at the bank.

"Yeah, maybe, but it's not my thing. I'm no penny pick-upper, if that's a word. But, 'to each his own'. I guess if some people are okay with it, then let them be. But it should also be okay for those of us who don't want to pick up pennies."

Copper felt sad, but it made sense. People had choices, and whether they chose to pick up or not pick up pennies, ought to be respected. The little coin was convinced that in some place and time, the right person would pick up its copper relatives, and this was fine for now.

The sand had become movable where Gina's shoe had played with it. By now Eileen had finished her cigarette and tossed the butt away. As the women rose to leave, Gina attempted to fill back the hole her shoe had scuffed. Looking down, she paused. This couldn't be happening again, but it was. There in the light sand laid another brown penny.

"It's your lucky day, Eileen," she grinned and pointed to the coin.

"For heaven's sakes," was Eileen's dry remark as she bent down to pick up the second treasure she had found that day.

"You know what, I bet there're tons of pennies in the sand," Eileen was already moving the dirt and her labour was rewarded as one more face showed itself. This one was dull and blackish in colour.

"Hey, watch this." Eileen dropped the penny on the loose sand and turned it in circles with the heel of her runner. Picking it up, she showed it to her friend. "Just rub it and the gunk goes."

Gina's interest was piqued. Eileen repeated the ritual on the other side, blew off the fine particles that was clinging to it, and with a satisfied smile, placed the penny now brighter than Copper, in her pocket. That was a neat trick.

Pleased at her friend's interest, Eileen offered some more information. "Near the parking meters in winter, lots of coins get dropped and no one digs in the snow when it's 40 below. So when the snow melts, you can find lots of money there. And at beaches, too. Also Gina, check your sofa. I'm telling you, these pennies add up."

little copper pennies

"I'm fine with the ones from my couch," Gina countered, "Now if I knew I'd find a vintage penny, maybe I'll pick one up, but for now I'll decline."

How well Eileen had articulated Copper's case. The little coin was an ambassador for Canada but had found its own ambassador. The ladies walked away. Eileen was three pennies richer and Copper had found someone who needed it as much as Sarah did.

Penny Fact

1. The 2002 penny is dated 1952-2002 on the portrait side to celebrate Queen Elizabeth II Golden Jubilee. Since dates are usually placed on the reverse side, at a glance, the coin appears to be undated.
2. Between 1982-1996, the penny took on a 12-sided shape and the shape of the maple leaf twig was altered to make identification easier for the visually impaired.
3. The coin reverted to the round design in 1997 as the 12-sided shape was difficult to plate.

Penny Fun

- Place dirty pennies in a vinegar and salt mixture, or lemon juice and salt, and watch them become clean.
- Shine pennies by rubbing them in loose sand with the heel of your shoe.

CHAPTER 15

A SLICE OF POP CULTURE

Copper is a penny that's about to retire. You may say that this is totally in keeping with any life cycle: all good things come to an end. Maybe so. Or maybe not. Especially if it is deeply embedded in popular culture, it's not so easy to change talk that been around for centuries.

Entrenched in the culture are quotations about pennies that stand in a class all by themselves. Those maxims cannot be replaced. So with the phasing out of the penny's presence, references to pennies that can be found throughout the Canadian culture are on marching orders. Pretty much like throwing out the baby with the bath water.

So what will your thoughts be worth now? A nickel? The packaging 'a nickel for your thoughts' just does not ring as smoothly as *a penny for your thoughts*. This adage has been the ageless expression when asking a quiet person what she is thinking.

Do you know anyone who passed away *without a penny to his name*? If so, you'd know that he was without any money or inheritance. Or have you invited your friend to lunch but she declined since she did not have a penny to her name? If you were really desperate for her listening ear, or simply are a good friend, you'd know she's broke and buy her a meal.

Has someone *showed up like a bad penny*? A person compared to a bad penny is generally considered worthless, in need or in trouble. His presence is usually a negative sign as he is not welcome. When saying someone will *show up like a bad penny*, you can bet that the person is sure to show up in the future.

Who dropped the penny? This reference is akin to a joke or point that you suddenly grasped, much like when a motionless machine comes to life when a penny is placed in the slot. This phrase is mostly used in a positive way to describe a problem that has been solved.

What about *in for a penny, in for a pound*? If you take chances, no doubt this saying has been thrown your way. The idea here is once you will be taking any kind of risk, you may as well take a big risk, and try to reap the bigger reward. To phrase it another way, if the penalty for a crime is similar to the penalty of a more severe crime, it makes sense to commit the more severe crime, and hope you get away with it. Many persons make a bad situation worse by comforting themselves with this saying, particularly if the repercussions are negative. The phrase is also interpreted that you intend to finish something you have started.[1]

Why does your financial advisor encourage that if you *look after the pennies, the dollars would look after themselves*? This idiom implies that you should not invest in deals, however small, if you are not willing to back it with serious money, because that is just as if you are throwing your money away.

little copper pennies

Do you know anyone who is *penny-wise, pound foolish*? This description applies to a person who is not willing to spend small amounts of money on useful items, but could very well spend large amounts for wasted or trivial things. She could be frugal with small sums but extravagant with large sums, and end up with little in the long run.

Has an item *cost a pretty penny*? Similar to the phrase 'cost an arm and a leg', this remark means that you paid a lot of money and the item is expensive.

Did you learn the rhyme '*Find a penny, pick it up. All day long you'll have good luck,*' as a kid? If so, you'll remember that many claim that finding pennies brings good luck, based on early beliefs that metals were a gift from the gods and so warded off evil. The phrase also finds roots in the idea that money symbolizes power.

A penny saved is a penny earned. This common saying speaks to the virtue of saving, as money that you save is more valuable than money that you spend now. Many people who pick up pennies often quote this saying.

What is it to feel like *a penny waiting for change*? Worthless or helpless? In the face of defeat or loss, this expression has been a figure of speech to show zero options.

How about being as *shiny as a penny*? Anyone who has pulled an all-nighter and looks none the worse in the morning, is worthy of this description. In general it implies looking fresh, bright and cheerful after an activity that should have been draining or wearisome.

If you wanted to *spend a penny*, <u>don't do it at the till</u>. This expression actually refers to using the toilet. This reference dates back to the days and countries where persons needed a penny to open the door of the toilet.

Have you worn a pair of *penny loafers*? These slip on shoes possess a tiny wedge on the top where pennies could be tucked in.[2] It could save you carrying a purse.

Who have not had two *pennies to rub together*? If you didn't, it implies that you are very poor. This maxim is often used to describe persons who might not be working.

When would someone be *cut off without a penny*? Incurring the wrath of a benefactor can cause someone to be cut off without a penny. The expression refers to ending someone's allowance, or failing to leave a family member an inheritance.

Is your contribution to the discussion *penny ante*? If so, then it is of little value or importance.[3]

Will you still be able to give your *two cents worth* anymore when the penny is gone? Adding your piece to a conversation best summaries this maxim.

Do you sometimes have to *pinch pennies*? If you have little money and show great care in spending it, or if you are unwilling to spend money overall, you may be pinching pennies.

Can investors still invest in *penny stocks*? Yes. Penny stocks, also known as cent stocks in some countries, are common shares of small public companies that trade at low prices and low market capitalization.[4]

Have you played *penny pitch*, *penny toss* or made *penny towers*? Many have had fun with penny games when they want to pass time, or are bored.

Will the young be interested in the beats of *Pennies from Heaven* by Johnny Burke and Arthur Johnston? Or the movie and TV series of the same name? Who'll be singing *Penny Lane* by the Beatles?

little copper pennies

Soon penny sayings may not be understood in Canada, and like the tide that recedes from the shore, they'll be drowned in the ocean of idioms and proverbs. If you are buying from a second hand store or a garage sale, be mindful that some useless junk will not be worth a *red cent*, a reference to the red copper finish,5 of the coin, as well as the trivial value of what is being purchased. Or worse, if the food was unappetizing at the restaurant, you will never have the opportunity to *tip a penny*.

Yes, Copper is a penny waiting for change. As it retires, it has no penny stocks, yet it will not have to pinch pennies. There'll be no way to play penny games as it is being cut off without a penny. To not show up as a bad penny is costing the little coin more than a pretty penny. Could be that Copper will walk down Penny Lane to be melted, and then immortalized as a Penny from Heaven.

Penny Fact

1. There have been 104 domestic mintages of the penny for circulation from 1908 to 2012.
2. Prior to 1908, all mintages of the Canadian penny were done at either the Royal Mint in London or the Heaton Mint in Birmingham, England.
3. The mint at Winnipeg serves 75 foreign governments and is expanding its operations to accommodate more countries.

Penny Fun

- Use pennies to entertain a child by him teaching to count or by making designs. (Be careful of swallowing hazards.)

- Create an accent on a wall with pennies.

CHAPTER 16

THE EULOGY

Dear Canada and Friends,

Many of us struggle with mixed emotions before the face of extinction. Extinction brought through the decision to rid the life of the one-cent piece.

For a large number, their appreciation has slowly given way to indifference over the years. For many others, an almost romantic connection to the coin fosters sadness and nostalgia at the abolition of the little cent.

For those of us who considered the penny as a friend in addition to a currency, commerce derides the sentiments of our hearts.

It was my honour to research the legacy of the humble copper coin, to be associated with its robust heritage, to trace its path from inception to demise. I have been privileged to share its richness in the lives of the older generations, to learn how it mushroomed into ever-expanding uses and pastimes. I have been inspired to capture the memories, the joys, and meanings of its possession.

I have seen the penny erode in value, heard debates and arguments in support and in rejection, among friends and with strangers. Now from the winter of 2013, the shiny copper, the only denomination of its colour, will be taken from us, never to be distributed again.

Many will fondly pay tribute to the penny as the workhorse of the currency system, a tribute born out of the recognition of the coin as the foundation for all money used in public service. Recognition that specific numbers of one cent pieces form the larger monetary denominations.

Many others will measure the price of its metallic composition: copper, zinc, steel, those changes driven by public accountability for profit. They have labelled it an inconvenience and a nuisance. They have judged it by its weight and unwieldiness, as useless at best. Or as a waste of time when counted at tills, or being rolled and processed.

For me, however, it is more pleasant and desirable to recall the penny during this time of its phasing out, as an ambassador serving its beloved Canada. Though lowly and humble, it was exalted in the wallets and purses of Prime Ministers, dignitaries, kings and queens. It travelled to other lands, where it was touched and examined with curiosity and interest.

What a precious treasure the penny is now and will be forever in the memories of many persons in this country. Who will choose to not forget those childlike respites provided with the purchase of a penny?

Penny candy. A penny in a cake. A penny in a fountain for a wish come true. A penny in your loafers for a telephone call.

Ingrained in the language, the penny has given depth and magnitude in nuggets of wisdom. A penny for your thoughts to draw out the pensive. A penny saved is a penny earned to those who pick up pennies. Or adding your two cents piece to a conversation.

The analogies and comparisons in cultures are like links on a chain that stretched over oceans. Only now its understanding will soon be lost in our country.

Introducing the decimal system, a subtle hint of Canada's own assertion, we must not forget the logos and words inscribed on the little coin. The stately head of the Queen ornately displayed on its obverse, and the maple leaves on its reverse. Its proclamation in letters '**1 CENT CANADA**' and its year of production.

Symbols that will march into the future.

Words that will not.

As a legacy of public service, it is a miniscule consolation for us that the removal of the penny does not spell an end to its service. It continues its responsibilities and remains alive in electronic transactions, debit and credit cards, and cheques.

All that the penny was created to do, it has delivered. It is written in indelible language in this book. For over a century, it was the acclaimed servant of the monetary domain, full of value, power and promise.

The penny's was a life of adventure - it travelled from place to place, moved from owner to owner.

Its service was one of excitement - the penny was escorted into parliamentary chambers, bedroom chambers and bathroom stalls. It was carried into brothels and crime scenes, unbidden. Into secret meetings and everywhere else, it could have been a copper spy.

Its function was one of teacher - the penny taught children to count and invited queries into its composition, and history engraved on its face.

Its contribution was one of keepsake - the penny was eagerly sought by collectors and accepted as souvenirs by visitors, and the last one produced on May 4th is at rest in a museum.

Its presence was one of meaning - the penny marked occasions and was not just money.

Its charge was one of pressure and change - the penny's composition was altered multiple times, its size reconfigured.

Its duty was one of convenience - useful up to a point.

Through summers and winters, sunsets and dawns, the penny served and was loved.

Friends, what comfort can I extend to your gloomy hearts today? What beyond the knowledge that the penny has given Canadian history a copper workhorse, which throughout 155 years has fortified the coffers of this nation and its people?

The penny paid for goods and services, supported the needy and assured the survival of many. From February next year, its pledge will be no more.

Now for the wider good of the country, it has been declared that the penny's useful days have passed, its tiny life squeezed by inflation's ruthless hand. Its final run complete, next winter, it will be summoned back to banks to be converted into another form.

To be recycled into its composite elements. Transformed from its little shape that attracted protests of its nuisances, the unassuming circle that met rejection and scorn from many in its last years. It makes no demand as to what embodiment the transformation should be, but goes to rest hoping that it will be beautiful and relevant.

little copper pennies

Every one of us knew the penny personally. We spent it, received it, touched it, counted it, picked it up, rolled it, emptied it, tossed it, forgot it, hated it and loved it. Loved its brilliance, its power, its charitable acts, its beauty, its symbolism.

We will miss the penny. It will be described in past tense to the next generations, silent in the hallowed sanctums of museums. Many of you may treasure its possession in hindsight of its erasure. In this epoch, it will never be truly erased for it may be tucked away in repositories of peanut butter jars, on shelves, under beds and in drawers.

Historians, collectors, sentimentalists, children, poor, and aging generation: mourn now more for yourselves than for it.

As in 1858 when molten metal created its being, molten metal will decimate its existence.

The penny has finished the race. It has fulfilled unto elimination, a privilege that was given from the year of its inauguration, until this twenty first century in 2013. Now it cannot be more than a burden on the balance sheet. It cannot accomplish what it once did in commerce. It cannot control its rising production costs, so it bids you farewell.

May its metals be recycled for a noble cause.

May the memories of the penny be perpetuated in our hearts as a symbol of patriotism for our country, an appreciation for our past, an insight into our future.

May its departure be an acceptance of faith that speaks to our own mortality that 'an ending to all fine things must be.'

Au Revoir, little penny.

APPENDIX 1

100 TRANSACTIONS ROUNDED OFF
An Experiment

Rounding prices up and down has been a concern of consumers since the news broke on March 29, 2012 that the penny was going to be removed from circulation. Some consumers believe they will lose, and retailers claim they stand to lose more. Who is right?

Before showing you the results of 100 actual transactions rounded off and whether there was a savings or loss for consumers, let's look at some opinions of consumers and retailers obtained through a Google search.[1]

Star Fire Wheel said: *As soon as store managers become aware of the details of the penny fiasco, you have to know that the price guns will all be working overtime to increase all their prices so they end in even multiples of five cents. Chain stores will be among the worst abusers, because they will make millions more, and, once they adjust the prices, you won't be able to tell that it has been increased to round it up. So now* *they round up the taxes at the end and the stores will be very happy.*

Three Eights comments: *"The 2012 federal budget states: "The government expects that businesses will apply rounding for cash transactions in a fair and transparent manner." Larger businesses will be doing so and not try to double dip on the rounding off. It's those small corner store businesses that will inevitably try to fraudulently cash in on it. It obviously won't be every business but some will. They will be upwards rounding off individual items and/or upwards rounding off before our 13% HST (in NB) is applied. Then, apply the 13% and round off upwards again. We'll have to keep track with a calculator at the cash register to make sure rounding off is really done like it is "requested" (not legally imposed by an act or law):*

"The rounding will not be done on single items but on the total bill of sale. If the price ends in a one, two, six, or seven it gets rounded down to 0 or 5; and rounded up if it ends in three, four, eight or nine." Yeah right! I bet all sales will now always mysteriously end in 3, 4, 8 and 9. We'll end up paying more in the end. I can see the fights at the cash registers too! Should be interesting.

Nlcsa1 responds: *"As a business owner, I personally find many of these comments regarding retailers rubbing their hands together like greedy children extremely insulting, not to mention ill-informed. In the long run, I can see no benefit to business, financially or otherwise. This will serve to ensure that more people will pay with methods other than cash, in order to ensure they get their money's worth... And rightfully so. But what many people don't seem to understand is that we, the business owners, will incur higher costs as a result. When* *people use plastic to pay, we are charged a percentage based fee for every transaction that we process by the card companies. We cannot recover that cost. While many of you think that we will raise prices to recoup those fees, do you understand that we will have to pay higher percentages based on that? Think what you must, but there are actually business owners that are decent human beings."*

Results:

Treating the one hundred sales as paid in cash, proved that there was a difference of 11 cents.

In this experiment, the customer lost 11 cents to the businesses.

For the analysis, all purchases were made between February 2012 - May 2012 in the provinces of Saskatchewan and Alberta, and include taxes. Prices were rounded up or down in keeping with information on the Royal Mint's website, which has been expressed by CBC News Canada as, "The rounding will not be done on single items but on the total bill of sale. If the price ends in a one, two, six, or seven it gets rounded down to 0 or 5; and rounded up if it ends in three, four, eight or nine." (See Appendix 2.)

The goods and services were grouped, as grouping shows more easily which category most frequent pur-chases were made, and where a person could be likely to lose/save pennies.

Cents shown in parentheses means a loss.

Items were bought and services paid for at forty one businesses listed below, and involved a variety of everyday bills and needs faced by the average Canadian consumer:

SUSAN HARRIS

American Apparel, Ardene, Banff Gondola, Best Western, Bluenotes, Boston Pizza, Canada Post, Canadian Tire, Coop Gas, Food and Agro/hardware outlets, Costco, Dairy Queen, Esso, Extra Foods, Fields, Home Hardware, Honda, Insurances, KFC, La Vie En Rose, McDonald's, Melville Advance, Payless Shoe Store, Pharmasave, Regis Salon, Restorex Flooring, Royal Drug Mart, Energy, Power, Telephone, Shoppers, Sobey's, Superstore, The Bay, Town Office, Toyota, Veterinary Clinic, Walmart , Xclusive Hair, Zellers.

#	Retail Goods & Services	$ Cash Total	Rounded Up or Down?	By how much -(cents)	Customer saved or lost?	Cumulative total saved or (lost)
1	Stamps	2.99	Up	.01	Lost	(.01)
2	Runners	21.99	Up	.01	Lost	(.02)
3	Pets	50.34	Up	.01	Lost	(.03)
4	Stationery	10.28	Up	.02	Lost	(.05)
5	Office Supp.	5.25	none			
6	Office Supp.	7.35	none			
7	Vehicle	47.55	none			
8	Vehicle	94.81	Down	.01	Saved	(.04)
9	Pharmacy	33.55	none			
10	Pharmacy	32.10	none			
11	Pharmacy	19.14	Up	.01	Lost	(.05)
12	Clothing	33.00	none			
13	Clothing	13.20	none			
14	Clothing	10.90	none			
15	Clothing	52.80	none			
16	Clothing	42.90	none			
17	Clothing	17.85	none			
18	Clothing	23.10	none			
19	Personal	9.84	Up	.01	Lost	(.06)
20	Personal	36.75	none			
21	Personal	32.31	down	.01	Saved	(.05)
22	Personal	64.24	Up	.01	Lost	(.06)
23	Personal	8.79	up	.01	Lost	(.07)
24	Personal	103.50	none			
25	Household	9.89	Up	.01	Lost	(.08)
26	Household	7.78	Up	.02	Lost	(.10)

little copper pennies

27	Household	34.23	Up	.02	Lost	(.12)
28	Household	26.36	Down	.01	Saved	(.11)
29	Household	50.93	Up	.02	Lost	(.13)
30	Household	135.86	Down	.01	Saved	(.12)
31	Household	23.01	Down	.01	Saved	(.11)
32	Household	58.51	Down	.01	Saved	(.10)
33	Household	16.63	Up	.02	Lost	(.12)
34	Household	9.89	Up	.01	Lost	(.13)
35	Gas	41.10	none			
36	Gas	14.98	Up	.02	Lost	(.15)
37	Gas	52.80	none			
38	Gas	53.00	none			
39	Gas	49.05	none			
40	Gas	47.00	none			
41	Gas	46.01	Down	.01	Saved	(.14)
42	Gas	50.42	Down	.02	Saved	(.12)
43	Gas	46.12	Down	.02	Saved	(.10)
44	Gas	45.00	none			
45	Gas	53.35	none			
46	Gas	48.16	Down	.01	Saved	(.09)
47	Gas	49.01	Down	.01	Saved	(.08)
48	Gas	47.00	none			
49	Recreation	40	none			
50	Recreation	19.29	Up	.01	Lost	(.09)
51	Recreation	160.41	Down	.01	Saved	(.08)
52	Recreation	28.10	none			
53	Recreation	17.93	Up	.02	Lost	(.10)
54	Recreation	13.62	Down	.02	Saved	(.08)
55	Recreation	18.80	none			
56	Recreation	11.73	Up	.02	Lost	(.10)
57	Recreation	107.65	none			
58	Recreation	22.37	Down	.02	Saved	(.08)
59	Recreation	19.29	Up	.01	Lost	(.09)
60	Recreation	4.71	Down	.01	Saved	(.08)
61	Recreation	13.18	Up	.02	Lost	(.10)
62	Recreation	10.49	Up	.01	Lost	(.11)
63	Recreation	75.38	Up	.02	Lost	(.13)
64	Recreation	9.49	Up	.01	Lost	(.14)
65	Bill	86.81	Down	.01	Saved	(.13)
66	Bill	100.00	none			
67	Bill	128.74	Up	.01	Lost	(.14)
68	Bill	10.99	Up	.01	Lost	(.15)

69	Bill	128.74	Up	.01	Lost	(.16)
70	Bill	64.12	Down	.02	Saved	(.14)
71	Bill	140.00	none			
72	Bill	68.00	none			
73	Bill	85.96	Down	.01	Saved	(.13)
74	Bill	59.12	Down	.02	Saved	(.11)
75	Bill	66.46	Down	.01	Saved	(.10)
76	Bill	23.36	Down	.01	Saved	(.09)
77	Bill	70.00	none			
78	Bill	70.00	none			
79	Bill	85.96	Down	.01	Saved	(.08)
80	Bill	180.79	Up	.01	Lost	(.09)
81	Groceries	36.56	Down	.01	Saved	(.08)
82	Groceries	243.86	Down	.01	Saved	(.07)
83	Groceries	59.02	Down	.02	Saved	(.05)
84	Groceries	36.75	none			
85	Groceries	84.15	none			
86	Groceries	24.87	Down	.02	Saved	(.03)
87	Groceries	33.68	Up	.02	Lost	(.05)
88	Groceries	50.65	none			
89	Groceries	11.62	Down	.02	Saved	(.03)
90	Groceries	124.53	Up	.02	Lost	(.05)
91	Groceries	35.26	Down	.01	Saved	(.04)
92	Groceries	32.58	Up	.02	Lost	(.06)
93	Groceries	13.75	none			
94	Groceries	136.19	Up	.01	Lost	(.07)
95	Groceries	115.26	Down	.01	Saved	(.06)
96	Groceries	62.38	Up	.02	Lost	(.08)
97	Groceries	3.18	Up	.02	Lost	(.10)
98	Groceries	213.06	Down	.01	Saved	(.09)
99	Groceries	219.88	Up	.02	Lost	(.11)
100	Groceries	53.35	none			

The Department of Finance has indicated that businesses are expected to round prices for cash transactions in a fair, consistent and transparent manner. It endorses that the experience in other countries that have eliminated low denomination coins, has shown that fair rounding practices have been respected.[2]

Since there is no watchdog to gauge that the practice is truly fair, the consumer cannot know if prices are rigged

little copper pennies

to reflect an upward rounding. The 2006 census noted that there were eight million, eight hundred and ninety six thousand, eight hundred and forty (8, 896,840) households in Canada.[3] More, if you consider kids living away from home to study or work.

If all these households lose 11 cents a year, that is close to a whopping one million dollars ($978, 652.40 to be exact.)

If the experiment is repeated it might produce different results, or not. Why don't you try it?

APPENDIX 2

Canada's penny withdrawal: All you need to know

(Reproduced by permission of CBC News Canada)

Making sense of the 1-cent coin's fate: FAQs

CBC News Posted: Mar 30, 2012 7:38 PM ET Last Updated: Apr 2, 2012 9:34 AM ET

What's up with the penny?

The government announced in the budget that it is eliminating the penny from Canada's coinage system. In about six months the Royal Canadian Mint will stop distributing Canadian coppers.

(Author's note - On July 30, 2012 the federal government announced that the Royal Canadian Mint will stop distributing pennies to financial institutions as of Feb. 4, 2013 as waiting until after the holiday shopping season would allow banks and businesses ample time to train staff and better inform consumers.)

What's going to happen to the pennies that are in circulation?

Starting in the fall, businesses will be asked to return pennies to financial institutions. The coins will be melted and the metal content recycled.

In the meantime, Canadians can continue to use pennies to pay for things and the one-cent piece will retain its value indefinitely.

How long will it take?

"There is no end date to this process," Alex Reeves of the Royal Canadian Mint told CBC News.

I want to empty my penny jar. How many pennies can be used for a purchase?

The Currency Act states: "A payment in coins ... is a legal tender for no more than ... 25 cents if the denomination is one cent."

How will we pay for things in amounts not ending in a zero or a five?

The 2012 federal budget states: "The government expects that businesses will apply rounding for cash transactions in a fair and transparent manner."

The rounding will not be done on single items but on the total bill of sale. If the price ends in a one, two, six, or seven it gets rounded down to 0 or 5; and rounded up if it ends in three, four, eight or nine.

Businesses will not need to adjust their cash registers.

little copper pennies

What about the sales tax and the GST/HST?

They won't make a difference. The government wants the rounding done on cash transactions only after the taxes have been added to the sub-total.

What about non-cash sales?

Cheques, credit and debit cards and electronic transactions will continue to be settled to the cent.

What's a penny worth?

The government says it costs 1.6 cents to produce each penny.

Adjusted for inflation, an 1870 penny would be worth about 31 cents today.

Why 1870 and how long have we been using pennies?

The first coins of the Dominion of Canada were issued in 1870, although the penny was not added until 1876. The penny had been in use in what is now Canada since 1858, when the province of Canada adopted the decimal system.

From 1858 to 1907, Canadian coins were struck at mints in England. The first Canadian-produced penny dates from 1908, when the Ottawa branch of the British Royal Mint opened.

Since 1908, the mint has produced 35 billion pennies, half of them in the last 20 years.

How many pennies are in circulation?

According to Alex Reeves, "given the extent of hoarding that has occurred for many years, it is not possible to accurately estimate the number of pennies still in circulation" and the mint does not reveal the number of coins removed from circulation.

Why does the government want to get rid of the penny?

The government says it costs about $11 million a year to supply pennies to the economy.

With other coins, the government says it "earns more from the sale of coins at face value than it pays to the mint for their production."

Those revenues should increase slightly after penny distribution ends, as demand for other coins should increase.

The minimum cost of keeping the penny in circulation was $150 million in 2006, according to the Desjardins Group. However, the cost that year would have been especially high because it was the peak year for penny production. The $150 million includes costs for government, financial institutions, retailers and consumers.

Will prices go up?

The government claims the inflationary effect of eliminating the penny will be small or non-existent, based on a study by the Bank of Canada in 2005.

Where is the penny produced?

Winnipeg.

little copper pennies

The copper penny was last produced in 1996.

Why do the letters KG appear on the penny below the maple leaf?

Those are the initials for George Edward Kruger Gray the English artist who created the penny's maple leaf twig design in 1937. His design, and his initials, also adorn the Canadian nickel.

Coins abandoned around the world

Other countries have stopped using their low-value coins. Some examples:

- Australia removed its one-cent and two-cent coins from circulation in 1992.
- Brazil discontinued the production of one-centavo coins in 2005.
- Finland has not issued one-cent or two-cent euro coins since the euro was introduced in 2002.
- Israel stopped issuing the one-agora coin in 1991 and the five-agorot coin in 2008.
- Netherlands stopped issuing one-cent and two-cent euro coins in 2004.
- New Zealand removed its one-cent and two-cent coins from circulation in 1989 and its five-cent coin in 2006.
- Norway removed its one-öre and two-öre coins in 1972; by 1991, it had also removed its five-, 10- and 25-öre coins.
- Sweden removed its one-öre and two-öre coins in 1971; by 1992, it had also removed its five-, 10- and

25-öre coins. In 2009, it removed the 50-öre coins from circulation.

- Switzerland officially withdrew its one-centime coin from circulation in 2006, while the two-centime coin lost its legal tender status in 1978.
- Britain removed the legal tender status of the half-penny in 1984.

Source: Department of Finance, Canada

So how many pennies are produced in a year?

(Author's note - The bar graph was not reproducible so the Author lists the numbers by year of mintage.)

The total amount of pennies produced in an average year weigh about 7,000 tonnes.

Mintages:

1908 - 1909

1908 - 2,401,506
1909 - 3,973,339

1910-1919

1910 - 5,146,487
1911 - 4,663,486
1912 - 5,107,642
1913 - 5,735,405
1914 - 3,405,958
1915 - 4,932,134
1916 - 11,022,367
1917 - 11,899,254

little copper pennies

1918 - 12,970,798
1919 - 11,279,634

1920-1929

1920 - 22,246,170
1921 - 7,601,627
1922 - 1,243,635
1923 - 1,019,022
1924 - 1,593,195
1925 - 1,000,622
1926 - 2,143,372
1927 - 3,553,928
1928 - 9,144,860
1929 - 12,159,840

1930-1939

1930 - 2,538,613
1931 - 3,842,776
1932 - 21,316,190
1933 - 12,079,310
1934 - 7,042,358
1935 - 7,526,400
1936 - 8,768,769
1937 - 10,090,231
1938 - 18,365,608
1939 - 21,600,319

1940-1949

1940 - 85,740,532
1941 - 56,336,011
1942 - 76,113,708

1943 - 89,111,969
1944 - 44,131,216
1945 - 77,268,591
1946 - 56,662,071
1947 - 74,949,349
1948 - 25,767,779
1949 - 33,128,933

1950-1959

1950 - 60,444,992
1951 - 80,430,379
1952 - 67,631,736
1953 - 67,806,016
1954 - 22,181,760
1955 - 56,403,193
1956 - 78,685,535
1957 - 100,601,792
1958 - 59,385,679
1959 - 83,615,343

1960-1969

1960 - 75,772,775
1961 - 139,598,404
1962 - 227,244,069
1963 - 279,076,334
1964 - 484,655,322
1965 - 304,441,082
1966 - 183,644,388
1967 - 345,140,645
1968 - 329,695,772
1969 - 335,240,929

little copper pennies

1970-1979

1970 - 344,145,010
1971 - 298,228,936
1972 - 451,304,591
1973 - 457,058,489
1974 - 692,058,489
1975 - 642,618,000
1976 - 701,122,890
1977 - 453,050,666
1978 - 911,170,647
1979 - 753,942,953

1980-1989

1980 - 911,800,000
1981 - 1,209,468,500
1982 - 876,036,898
1983 - 975,510,000
1984 - 838,225,000
1985 - 771,772,500
1986 - 788,285,000
1987 - 774,549,000
1988 - 482,676,752
1989 - 1,066,628,200

1990-1999

1990 - 218,035,000
1991 - 831,001,000
1992 - 673,512,000
1993 - 808,585,000
1994 - 639,516,000
1995 - 624,983,000

1996 - 445,746,000
1997 - 549,868,000
1998 - 999,578,000
1999 - 1,089,625,000

2000 - Present

2000 - 902,506,000
2001 - 928,434,000
2002 - 830,040,000
2003 - 748,123,000
2004 - 842,486,000
2005 - 767,425,000
2006 - 1,261,883,000
2007 - 846,420,000
2008 - 787,625,000
2009 - 455,680,000
2010 - 486,200,000
2011 - 662,750,000

Source: The Royal Canadian Mint

(Author's note - mintage numbers for 2012 will be available in 2013.)

ENDNOTES & ADDITIONAL READING

Chapter 2 - The Maple leaf

1. Stanley Cup History, http://proicehockey.about.com/od/stanleycupbunker/a/stanley_cup.htm

2. Maple Syrup FAQ, http://www.mississauga.ca/portal/discover/educationprograms?paf_gear_id=9700018&itemId=4400174&returnUrl=%2Fportal%2Fdiscover%2Feducationprograms

3. The Maple Leaf, http://www.pch.gc.ca/pgm/ceem-cced/symbl/o3-eng.cfm

Chapter 3 - In the Fountain

1. Celtic Twilight, http://www.celtic-twilight.com

Read more at http://www.winnipegfreepress.com/local/mint-to-stamp-out-canadas-last-penny-this-morning-150132465.html

Read more at http://www.mint.ca/store/dyn/PDFs/RollTimeline_e.pdf

Chapter 4 - The Coins in the Locomotive

1. CN North America's Railroad, http://www.cn.ca

Chapter 5 - Around the House

Read more in Appendix 2 or at Canada's penny withdrawal:
All you need to know at http://www.cbc.ca/news/canada/
story/2012/03/30/f-penny-faq.html?cmp=rss

Chapter 6 - The Collection and a Biker

1. Mint will stop making pennies this fall, http://money.ca.msn.
   com/federalbudget/mint-will-stop-making-pennies-this-fall

Chapter 7 - The Penny in the Cake

Read more at The Royal Canadian Mint Currency Timeline, http://
www.mint.ca/store/dyn/PDFs/RollTimeline_e.pdf

Read more at 1858 penny, http://www.canadiancoinsdollar.
com/1858-Canada-Large-Canadian -Pennies.html.

Chapter 8 - The Ole Days

1. Centum, http://www.urbandictionary.com/define.php?term=
   centum%20(latin%20for%20100)

Read more at http://www.coinsite.com/content/articles/Cana-
daSilver.asp

Chapter 9 - More of the Good Ole Days

Read more at http://www.vancouversun.com/business/Photos+Ca
nadian+Penny+1858+2012/6382183/story.html

Chapter 10 - Grade Five

Read more in Appendix 2 or at Canada's penny withdrawal:
All you need to know at http://www.cbc.ca/news/canada/
story/2012/03/30/f-penny-faq.html?cmp=rss

Chapter 11 - High School Debate

1. Backgrounder: Withdrawing the Penny from Circulation. http://www.parkpennies.com/penny/end-canadian-penny.htm

2. Öre no more...http://www.nordstjernan.com/news/nordic/2694/

3. Royal Mint Australia. When were 1c & 2c coins taken out of circulation? http://www.ramint.gov.au/faq/

4. Eliminating the Penny, http://www.actionplan.gc.ca/en/backgrounder/eliminating-penny

5. Currency Act, http://laws.justice.gc.ca/eng/acts/C-52/page-1.html

Chapter 12 - The Retailers Meeting

1. Eliminating the penny. What it means for businesses http://www.mint.ca/store/mint/learn/what-it-means-for-businesses

2. Penny's life extended to Feb. 4 http://www.cbc.ca/news/business/story/2012/07/30/penny-end-date.html

3. http://tires.canadiantire.ca/view/content/genericContents?pageid=tireTreadDepth

Chapter 13 - D.G. and other Symbolic Meanings

1. A National Symbol - the 1-cent coin, http://www.mint.ca/store/mint/learn/1-cent-5300004

2. Elemental Alchemy Symbol, http://www.whats-your-sign.com/elemental-alchemy-symbols.html

3. Periodic Table: Copper, http://www.chemicalelements.com/elements/cu.html

4. The Royal Canadian Mint Currency Timeline, http://www.mint.ca/store/dyn/PDFs/RollTimeline_e.pdf

5. George V 1911-1936, http://www.calgarycoin.com/modern/cdcent.htm

Chapter 14 - Picking up Pennies

Read more at http://www.mint.ca/store/dyn/PDFs/RollTimeline_e.pdf

Chapter 15 - A Slice of Popular Culture

1. In for a penny in for a pound, http://dictionary.reference.com/browse/in+for+a+penny,+in+for+a+pound

2. Penny Loafers, http://www.valetmag.com/style/profiles-features/2011/anatomy-of-a-classic-penny-loafer.php

3. Penny ante, http://www.thefreedictionary.com

4. Penny Stock, http://www.canadian-money-advisor.ca/what-is-buying-penny-stocks.html

5. Red cent, http://dictionary.reference.com/browse/red+cent

Appendix 1 - 100 Transactions

1. Canada's penny withdrawal: All you need to know, http://www.cbc.ca/news/canada/story/2012/03/30/f-penny-faq.html?cmp=rss

2. Eliminating the penny. What it means for businesses, http://www.mint.ca/store/mint/learn/what-it-means-for-businesses

3. 2006 Census: Families, marital status, households and dwelling characteristics, http://www.statcan.gc.ca/daily-quotidien/070912/dq070912a-eng.htm

Penny images

Read more at

http://www.ottawacitizen.com/business/Photos+Canadian+Penny+1858+2012/6381634/story.html

http://www.vancouversun.com/business/Photos+Canadian+Penny+1858+2012/6382183/story.html

ABOUT THE AUTHOR

 Susan Harris is a dreamer, speaker and educator. A high school teacher for twelve years, she transferred those skills from the classroom to the pulpit and into organizations. Now she continues to educate through the medium of formal writing.

Creating memories, preserving the past and learning new things have been her lifelong passion, and her creative and childlike imagination brings freshness to mundane topics and trivial passing.

Susan is the author of *Golden Apples in Silver Settings: Words that have inspired audiences in snowy and sunny lands.* Now her words capture the journey of the retired Canadian penny in *little copper pennies: Celebrating the life of the Canadian one-cent piece (1858-2013).*

Susan obtained her Bachelor of Science in Management Studies from the University of the West Indies in 1988, and then completed a post graduate Diploma in Education. She went on to earn a Certificate in Theology from the West Indies School of Theology, and a Certificate in Writing from the Institute of Literature in Connecticut. As a professional, she holds the designation of Certified Human Resources Professional in Canada.

Born and raised in the small, sunny island of Trinidad, she lives in Saskatchewan's smallest city of Melville with her husband, daughter, and Smokey the larger than life cat.

Contact Susan Harris at http://susanharris.ca

Find Susan on Facebook at www.facebook.com/goldensusanharris

Follow Susan on Twitter @SusanHarris20

Email Susan at susan@susanharris.ca

OTHER BOOKS BY SUSAN HARRIS

Coming soon - *little copper pennies for KIDS* picture book

Golden Apples in Silver Settings: Words that have inspired audiences in snowy and sunny lands

Overtaxed schedules, increasing responsibilities and multiple demands often result in Christians being unable to attend church or retreats, and they become concerned about what they may have missed. That concern should be dispelled by **Golden Apples in Silver Settings** (http://www.goldenapplesinsilversettings.com), which invites persons to experience God in a variety of locations without leaving the comfort of their favourite chair. One can attend a conference without taking time off work or paying registration fees.

Susan Harris, the author, is a speaker, previous teacher and writer (http://www.susanharris.ca) whose spiritual and educational background – in Theology, Management, Education, Human Resources and Sales - enabled her to inspire and encourage thousands through the 20 messages she shares. While some of them aren't thought of as new topics, the practical empowerment and Biblical insights are key factors for success in encouraging the reader. For example:

- The person who fears the night can take comfort from the knowledge that God keeps the night watch.

- The woman who needs to be restored can model on Rahab, who in spite of her past occupied a place of prominence, and her name is written in the Hall of Fame in a place called Eternity.

- The man who desires the peace of his Christian neighbour can know the gospel of Jesus.

Many of the messages can be understood by persons with or without a biblical background or church affiliation. Some — for example, *Turning Dreams Into Reality* — is relevant to anyone. Some readers may be motivated to forgive, or pray, or increase faith, and some may experience healing. Most of the principles can be springboards for discussions and study, or transferable concepts to encourage others.

As Harris unfolds each message, readers will:

- Learn strategies for restoration and hope

- Be empowered to dream and live those dreams

- Engage through the conversational style of "Dear Friend"

- Understand the Christian faith in a clear and simple manner

- Be able to imagine themselves in the audience, city, town or island where the message was given

In the pages, readers will be transported to silver settings in the Caribbean and Canada, and be energized with truth as timeless as golden apples — Proverbs 25:11. Themes tailored to specific areas including passion, favour, breakthrough, freedom, victory, prayer, thanksgiving, healing, seasons, restoration, love, salvation and joy, enable readers in identifying the most relevant ones that would have would have greatest impact on their immediate need.

While there are many books providing faith and encourage-ment, Harris gives fresh meaning to the term "Christian Author and Speaker," demonstrating that a trained professional's knowledge, experience and dependence on God offers valued treasure to those who are also dependent on God.

Buy this ebook at http://www.amazon.com/ Golden-Apples-Silver-Settings-ebook

Or at http://www.smashwords.com/books/view/145387

ISBN 978-0-9868928-1-3

Buy a print copy at

- http://www.goldenapplesinsilversettings.com

little copper pennies

- or at the website http://www.susanharris.ca
  ISBN 978-0-9868928-0-6

Find Susan on Facebook at www.facebook.com/goldensusanharris

Follow Susan on Twitter @SusanHarris20

Contact Susan Harris by email at susan@susanharris.ca